**Knowledge
Exploitation Fund**

Cronfa Datblygu
Gwybodaeth

- 4 OCT 2002

GETTING STARTED IN IMPORTING

**Knowledge
Exploitation Fund**

Cronfa Datblygu
Gwybodaeth

BUSINESS *ENTERPRISE*

*G*ETTING *S*TARTED IN *I*MPORTING

A Practical Guide

John R Wilson

**KOGAN
PAGE**

The masculine pronoun has been used throughout this book. This stems from a desire to avoid ugly and cumbersome language, and no discrimination, prejudice or bias is intended.

First published in 1996
Second edition 1998

Kogan Page Limited
120 Pentonville Road
London Nl 9JN

British Library Cataloguing in Publication Data

A CIP record for this book is available from the British Library.

ISBN 0 7494 2818 X

Typeset by Saxon Graphics Ltd, Derby
Printed and bound in Great Britain by Clays Ltd, St Ives plc

Contents

Contents

Contents

Acknowledgements

Information and help was provided by friends, colleagues and the following organizations: British International Freight Association, The Crafts Council, Customs and Excise, EMIC Library, Department of Industry, Laytons, international trade lawyers, Oldfire Ltd, Praed Street Business Services (Helen and Jenny), Simpler Trade Procedures Board.

1

Introduction

This book is intended to help anyone who is interested in developing directly or indirectly a business that wishes to extend its purchases to include imported goods or services. It will help them to find and evaluate new possible sources of supply, overcome problems and exploit opportunities. A knowledge of the cost of a product at source is not sufficient. It is essential to know the additional costs of bringing it to your premises and how you or your supplier might keep these to the minimum. This book will be of use not only to those people in small and medium-sized enterprises but also to those interested in importing in larger companies.

Many exporters will also find this book useful as it should help them to understand the views and problems of importers. It is doubtful if you can be a really successful importer without such knowledge. It is most important that buyers and suppliers have a reasonable understanding of each other's businesses, particularly their methods of international trading.

Many people will claim that, whereas it is easy to do business with companies in developed countries, it is not so simple in developing countries. If you are trying to do regular business with a country with a poor transport infrastructure, an inefficient banking system and which is also not quality conscious, it is likely to be difficult. Unfortunately, some developing countries erect banking and other obstacles to overseas trade, although these usually affect their exporters as much as their importers. Such difficulties can usually be overcome by skill and ingenuity.

Importing is not difficult from a country with a freely exchangeable and stable currency and well-structured financial, industrial and service sectors, including good transport facilities and few other obstacles to overseas trade. If a company chooses wisely where and how to start trading or where to expand its business, business relations should be much less difficult than expected.

Purchasing skills are important in most businesses and they do determine the success or failure of many small companies. It is not sufficient to have a knowledge of purchasing only in the UK if you really wish to succeed in the international field. Gaining new knowledge and extra skills in importing by experience only can be very costly.

It is very easy to become an importer or to enlarge your overseas contacts and suppliers simply by attending fairs and exhibitions and buying at them. It is much better first to acquire a knowledge of importing by reading suitable books and magazines and by attending seminars run by such organizations as Chambers of Commerce and the Chartered Institute of Purchasing and Supply. If you intend to employ somebody to do all your importing, it is still important to have sufficient knowledge of international trade to enable you to have sensible and meaningful discussions with that person. Even if you deal with an independent wholesaler from whom you buy imported goods, it is always useful to have a knowledge of international trade. Should he make excuses for supply or communication failures you may be able to judge whether they are genuine and suggest better alternatives.

RESEARCH MARKETS AND SUPPLIERS

The biggest problem for importers is to ensure that they are dealing with reliable suppliers. If not, they may find themselves paying for goods of inferior quality and experiencing late deliveries. To some extent it is the responsibility of the importer to establish purchasing conditions with his supplier and not just tamely to accept the supplier's sales conditions. It is particularly important to have clear specifications for goods and packaging as well as clearly agreed arrangements on payments and insurance. It is in the importer's best interests not to have to pay for the goods until he has taken the title to them and inspected them. This enables him to check that the goods have arrived in good condition and are as ordered, before he pays.

As an importer it is important to identify the key markets and suppliers that could be interested in meeting your requirements. It is then necessary to determine if the goods can be used profitably either in your manufacturing process or for resale. There is no sense in wasting time, money and effort in pursuing possible goods or services from overseas markets unless they will enable you to achieve a satisfactory profit. There are a number of different ways in which you can carry out some quick market research to determine where to concentrate your efforts, which are described later. It is a mistake to drift into importing as there is a good possibility that you will not get the best deal in terms of either quality, price or delivery. By far the best way to become an importer or to extend your importing activities is to have a carefully thought out plan of action to achieve your objectives.

Many of the information services available in the UK are designed primarily to assist exporters; however, a lot of it is of assistance to importers. Central libraries, major banks, government departments, professional institutes, trade associations and Chambers of Commerce provide information, much of which is often free. Some of them also provide training in importing and organize other events such as purchasing seminars which often include some aspects of international purchasing.

Importers who wish to establish a close relationship with their suppliers in a non-English-speaking country will find it particularly helpful to acquire some skills in the appropriate foreign language as well as an understanding of the culture of that country. Language and cultural barriers cause some firms to buy from middlemen rather than obtain their requirements direct from the supplier in the overseas market. The importance of the single market in Europe is such that many more people now need to learn foreign languages for business purposes so that they can participate directly in international trade.

SMALL FIRMS

A small firm wishing to import goods or services should find that its local enterprise agency, Training and Enterprise Council (TEC) and local Business Link shop can give advice and help. The local central library should also be a good source for information and books on importing, particularly if it is a business library or has a good business section. Excise and Inland Customs Advice Centres are able to provide all the information and leaflets relating to UK duties and taxes on the goods you may wish to import. If, instead of importing directly from overseas suppliers, you wish to purchase from sources in the UK, it will be necessary to find a wholesaler or distributor. Information on possible suppliers can be obtained from various sources such as directories.

BUYING DIRECT FROM SUPPLIERS

Once possible overseas suppliers have been identified, enquire if they have agents or distributors in the UK. If the answer is in the affirmative, they will almost certainly require you to buy through them; however, if your business is sufficiently large, they may be willing to trade with you directly. Even if the UK agent or distributor is a wholly or partly owned subsidiary of their company, they may still be willing to deal with you partly or wholly on a direct basis. It is a mistake to assume you will necessarily get better terms or a superior service by buying direct. The agent or distributor will probably receive a commission on your purchases whether or not he is directly involved in your transaction. In any case, he will probably intervene if any problems arise over quality, delivery, payments or service.

There are other ways of finding possible suppliers and these will be covered in Chapter 2.

WHOLESALING OR RETAILING

Anyone wishing to become an importer may have the choice of being a distributor, an independent wholesaler or a retailer. A distributor normally has a formal arrangement with an overseas supplier to act as his stockist and sales force in the market. The distributor may act for more than one supplier provided the products from different suppliers do not compete with one another. There is some advantage if they are complementary products and purchased by the same customers. For example, orders for a variety of products will probably be large and require less sales effort for each unit of sales.

An independent wholesaler is one who is not tied to any particular supplier and ideally obtains his goods from the best and cheapest suppliers anywhere in the world. He has to be continually on the alert for new suppliers and new product opportunities for sales in the market sectors in which he operates. As an independent buyer he will have more freedom and should not be constrained by the overseas supplier as to the prices at which he sells. In general, he does not need to give his overseas suppliers information on his market and price mark-ups. A tied distributor will undoubtedly have to provide such information to his supplier, ie his principal, probably to the extent of having to send monthly reports on sales, and to open his books to him.

Should you wish to be a *retailer* of imported goods you may have the choice of importing them direct or buying from the UK distributors of overseas suppliers or in some cases independent importers. Buying them in the UK avoids the problems associated with importing; however, one may find that the price is higher than if you import direct from the overseas supplier. The fruit, flower and vegetable trade is a very good example of exported goods being sold through wholesalers in the wholesale fruit and vegetable markets. The majority of retailers of such products in the UK will buy their produce from the wholesale markets. However, for some products the large supermarkets deal directly with major overseas suppliers provided they can be confident that the quality of the goods, packaging and service will at all times meet their specifications.

Industrial users of imported products are most likely to buy them through the UK agents of the overseas manufacturers. The goods will be delivered directly from the overseas supplier to your specified destination and the goods will have to be paid for in accordance with the agreed payment terms.

It will be apparent that, according to the type of products you wish to import, you can be a tied distributor, an independent wholesaler, a retailer or an agent. In addition, depending on the type of service and products you wish to offer, you may be able to obtain a franchise, negotiate a licence to manufacture the goods in the UK and even perhaps enter into a joint venture or business cooperation arrangement with the overseas company. It is worth exploring all these possibilities to see which option is of most interest to you.

PACKAGING AND LABELLING

The packaging and labelling of products by the exporter has to be of a high standard in accordance with regulatory requirements and must provide protection against damage and pilferage. If the importer is buying on an ex-works basis, he must himself see that all these requirements are met although he may decide to appoint a freight forwarder in the overseas country to look after those matters and to arrange shipment. Your decision will depend on how the goods are to be sent to the UK, the nature of the goods and your own expertise. If goods are coming from a country in the single market, the problems are likely to be fewer than if they are coming from deep sea markets.

If you are importing goods for resale, you also have to consider how they should be packed to assist with the sales and promotion of the goods in the UK. You may wish to buy them in bulk and repackage them yourself or arrange for the overseas supplier to see that each individual item is packaged and labelled in accordance with your needs and UK regulations. If you repackage the items yourself, as you might do with imported textiles, you can use UK package designers to design attractive packaging for you. The Design Council provides a list of names of suitable designers. A walk round any supermarket or department store looking at packaging and labelling shows how important it is to get this right in order to promote the sale of your goods.

In determining your start-up costs it is essential to take into account designers' fees and other setting-up charges for the packaging and labelling. It is then important to determine the actual package cost for each item unless it is included in the supplier's price. Addresses of the organizations mentioned in the text which the reader may need to contact are given in Chapter 12, Further Information.

2

Researching Sources of Supply

One of the most important tasks for any potential importer is to find suppliers who can meet his requirements and those of his customers. Most potential importers have very clear ideas of the type of product or products they wish to import. They will probably be aware of similar products available in the UK from local manufacturers or importers. If not, they should find out about the products that are already on the market. Should it be a product completely new to the UK, it is important to determine where it fits into the market. There is very little point in importing products until you have satisfied yourself that there is a market for them and that you know how to sell in your chosen market sector. As part of your research you may wish to import trial quantities to test the market, but this presupposes you have already found a satisfactory source of supply and that is not always easy.

SOURCES OF SUPPLY IN THE UK

Many reputable overseas manufacturers and producers are represented in the UK by agents, distributors and importing companies. Some of these may be subsidiary or associate companies of an overseas manufacturer. In the commodity field, in particular, there are many specialist importers of products such as flowers, fruit and vegetables, as well as those who import large volumes of products such as timber, coal and metals. To locate some of these importers it may only be necessary to look in business telephone directories; more often you will need to consult trade directories, such as the Directory of Importers, Kompass Country Directories and others. These give information on most types of imported product whether industrial or retail.

SOURCES OF SUPPLY OVERSEAS

Should you be unable to find a source of supply in the UK you have to search for suppliers overseas. It will be necessary to locate suppliers who are reliable and financially sound. Having found them, it will be up to you to agree prices, methods of payment, periods of credit, packaging, labelling and delivery arrangements. You may also wish to protect yourself against possible supply failures by having more than one source of supply. There is also the problem of exchange rate risks if you are paying in the supplier's currency. These are some of the factors that have to be taken into consideration when deciding where you are going to obtain your goods. Suppliers in developed countries such as those in Western Europe, North America, Japan, Australia and New Zealand are likely to be more reliable than those in developing countries. Markets in developed countries are more sophisticated and competitive. Suppliers are generally used to meeting the needs of customers whose standards are high.

SOURCES OF INFORMATION

The Department of Trade and Industry's (DTI) publication 'Overseas Trade Statistics' helps to identify countries which export the goods or services which you wish to import. The 'Trade and Navigation Accounts' and other individual country statistics enable you to identify the levels of imports and exports of products by individual country. These are very good guides to the main supplying countries. In turn, you can look at individual country trade directories to identify suppliers of the products required. All this information is available in the DTI's Export Market Information Centre (EMIC) library at the DTI's offices in Victoria Street, London; other libraries such as those in the larger Chambers of Commerce will also hold some of this information.

Some trade associations, particularly those whose members are engaged in international trade, should be able to supply details of overseas suppliers of materials and products which are not available in the UK but which may be used by their members. International trade magazines in the UK and foreign trade magazines will be a valuable source of information provided they specialize in the type of products in which you are interested. Copies of a country's various trade magazines may be available in the commercial sections of overseas embassies. Such sections are usually very helpful in providing information on exporters from their own country and many will advise these exporters of your interest in their products. A number of countries, such as Hong Kong and Singapore, have trade development organizations with branches in the UK which provide trade directories and more detailed information on suppliers' products and services.

A number of countries such as the USA also publish buyers' guides which are updated annually or more frequently. If you are looking for new products not yet introduced to the UK market, these guides can be a useful source of information.

Many international trade fairs are held in the UK and overseas where leading manufacturers display their goods. Information on international fairs is available from the DTI, Export Services Directorate, although they primarily serve UK exporters. There is also a *Directory of International Trade Fairs and Exhibitions* which potential importers may find useful. However, before visiting a fair, it is sensible to make enquiries within the trade to ensure that it is well established and supported by major suppliers. Attending a trade fair or exhibition is one very good way of meeting potential suppliers; it also enables you to compare similar products from different manufacturers.

Foreign Chambers of Commerce in the UK such as the Netherlands – British Chamber of Commerce and the American Chamber of Commerce (UK) are valuable sources of information on suppliers, trade fairs and other trade matters relating to business with the country they represent; in general, if you wish to do business with any of their members, they will supply initial information without charge. However, if you wish to import regularly from a particular country, you may find it beneficial to join their Chamber of Commerce in the UK.

Should you be interested in buying goods produced by small industries and craftsmen in developing countries, advice should be sought from the Developing Countries Trade Agency known as DECTA.

The Internet is an increasingly important source of information on potential suppliers of goods and services, particularly from developed countries. Goods can be bought and paid for via the Internet. Almost all UK importers are likely to be connected to the Internet by the next millennium.

SELECTING SUPPLIERS

Once you have a list of potential suppliers you need to ask for quotations. In making these requests it is essential to ask for or give specifications for the products you require and request any special requirements in respect of packaging, labelling and delivery. If you have your own purchasing conditions, you should attach a copy of these to your request for a quotation. Potential suppliers should also be asked to send you copies of their sales and technical literature and samples, where relevant. If you can give an indication of the quantities you are likely to want, frequency of deliveries and possible growth of your business, this will encourage suppliers to make a realistic quotation, especially if they grant discounts or rebates for minimum quantities.

Once you have received offers from various suppliers, either in one country or from various countries, you must decide which supplier or suppliers best meet your needs. At this stage you may also need to check the supplier's specification to see if it meets UK standards. The

British Standards Institution can assist you with most manufactured goods, regardless of whether or not they are for industrial use or for sale to retail consumers. If you import products that do not meet UK standards, particularly in respect of health and safety regulations, you may find you are unable to sell them.

Should you wish to act as an official agent or distributor for a supplier who already sells in the UK without representation, you should find out about him from existing purchasers of his goods in the UK. Some suppliers, for example of spare parts for the motor trade, may voluntarily provide information, giving names of some of their existing customers in the UK. If they do not currently sell in the UK, you may wish to consider becoming their UK agent or distributor, thus entering into a formal agreement with them to promote the sale of their products.

Assuming you have identified suitable suppliers you will wish to check further on their financial viability. Some of the major UK clearing banks may be able to provide you with information on overseas companies. Alternatively, you may be able to obtain the information from one of the credit rating agencies such as Dun & Bradstreet.

VISITING SUPPLIERS

It is desirable to visit potential suppliers before finally placing orders with them, especially as you may wish to try to negotiate better prices and delivery terms. Visits to potential suppliers in Western Europe present no real problems but to go further afield requires more time and money. In general, importers placing small orders do not visit overseas suppliers unless they have other reasons for visiting their country. However, if you are entering into a large contract or intending to sign an agency or distribution agreement for the UK then, if at all possible, the supplier's premises, his works and offices should be visited. This will enable you to assess the business and meet the people with whom you will be in regular contact.

PLANNING THE VISIT

Every time you visit an overseas market, plan your trip in advance, making sure you have confirmed appointments with all your existing suppliers and potential suppliers that you wish to meet. Since you are the buyer, and particularly if you are an important buyer, the supplier will probably assist you with your visit arrangements. He may recommend where to stay, make a hotel booking for you and arrange for a car to take you to his office or works. If you visit a market as part of a trade mission, many of these arrangements will be made by the visit organizers.

Travel within Western Europe is relatively easy, especially if you equip yourself with information on the country and the town you are visiting before your departure. Much of this information can be obtained from the country's tourist office in London. Even on arrival you should be able to obtain a town map and other information from the local tourist office. If you are going to countries further afield, especially developing countries, you will not find the same information so readily available, so make sure you use a reliable travel agent with representatives in the countries you propose to visit. Things do go wrong from time to time on overseas business trips and the travel company's representatives and the supplier you are visiting should be willing to help you. Make sure you have addresses and telephone numbers of people to contact in an emergency. The British Embassy will also advise and possibly help if you are faced with a really serious situation.

Your travel agent should be able to advise you about the documents, eg visas, that you may require. They should also warn you of the health risks and which inoculations are compulsory and which are desirable. The British Airways Travel Clinics (see phone book) and a number of other specialist organizations will give you good advice on what protection you need and what medication to take with you. Your doctor should have leaflets explaining what protection is needed for each country. He can also arrange inoculations, anti-malaria tablets and any other medication that you may require. Keeping fit is vital if you intend to have a successful visit.

A good travel agent will be able to advise you about clothing requirements, eg for very hot or very cold countries, and travel to and from your arrival point. Unfortunately, in some developing countries, unless your travel agent's representative meets you at the hotel, you might find the reception will claim they have no booking for you. Hotels do get overbooked and are taken over at short notice for important visiting parties of dignitaries and you need the help of the travel agent's representative in such situations. In developed countries it is not usually necessary to have this assistance but in some developing countries it is essential.

It is vital to have traveller's cheques for visit expenses and cash in local currency, assuming it is freely exchangeable on the world's currency markets. Clearly, Western European countries, North America, Japan and other developed countries are unlikely to present any real problems. In some developing countries with exchange controls you need to know about exchange rates before you arrive and any problems you are likely to have changing traveller's cheques and paying hotel bills in hard currency. It may not be easy to change traveller's cheques at any hour of the day or night and you may need to change money at your point of arrival. Since you are intending to purchase goods or services or at least enter into business arrangements during your visit you should know the sterling exchange rate and the structure of the local currency before you arrive. This knowledge will also enable you to make price comparisons with the goods and services being sold locally.

MEETING SUPPLIERS

The first meeting with a potential supplier is likely to be an exploratory meeting. If you act simply as a buyer, your negotiations will be much easier than if you try to have yourself appointed as his official agent or distributor. In a simple buying situation, you will be negotiating such matters as prices, payment terms, delivery terms, product specifications, packaging and labelling. If you are seeking an agency or distributor agreement, you will also need to discuss the clauses the supplier wishes to include in the agreement and those you wish to have inserted. You will also want to visit your supplier's premises and he yours before any agreement is signed.

Subsequent meetings with the supplier will depend on how important you are to each other. You will be seeking information from one another on the progress of existing business and any new developments. The supplier will want to know how you are developing the sales of his product, how it compares with competition and whether there is any customer resistance to the product, eg for price or quality reasons. You may want to discuss such matters as prices, delivery performance and any new or improved products that the supplier is introducing. Before attending such meetings it is advisable to draw up a list of items you wish to discuss, possibly sending a meeting agenda to your supplier beforehand. Naturally, you should take any relevant documents to the meeting plus any samples of packages, competitive products, etc that you may wish to discuss. The better both parties prepare for such meetings the more likely they will be successful.

3

International Trade and Payments

SUPPLIERS' RELIABILITY

The importer, ie the buyer, needs to ensure that he receives his goods on time and to his requirements; the supplier wants to make sure he receives payment on time. Each party wishes to know that the other is reliable. Some suppliers will only supply goods if they receive part payment with the order and the remaining payment when the goods are ready for despatch. This particularly applies to very small businesses in the craft and design field but many other firms will refuse to give credit to a buyer on an initial order. In any case, the supplier will wish to check the buyer's creditworthiness before granting credit. The importer will wish to check that he is dealing with a reliable and trustworthy supplier before placing orders. The importer and the supplier need to build a good relationship if both parties are to benefit from the business.

The importer should always be on the alert for a supplier running into production or financial difficulties. This could be indicated by slow deliveries, a deterioration in quality or by a change in normal business relations.

Mention has already been made of how to check the creditworthiness of a company. In developed countries there are many organizations that will, for a fee, provide a credit rating and other financial information on a company. Dun & Bradstreet are one of the best-known multinational companies in this field. They offer business information and other services. CCN Group are another UK firm who supply similar information and can be contacted direct or accessed via the Europe Network Ltd database. Another company providing such information is Graydon UK Ltd, who cover companies in over 160 countries.

Your clearing bank can also often provide a status report on a possible supplier. This is known as a *bank reference* and gives information on the creditability of a possible supplier. Should you wish to investigate the banks' credit assessment services in more detail you will find most of these organizations with stands at the Credit Management Exhibition, usually held in April at the Brewery, Chiswell Street, London or at the International Trade Exhibition, 'Intrade', held in London in June. A visit to both these exhibitions usually provides much useful information as well as an opportunity to talk to people very much involved in obtaining and supplying information about companies.

TERMS OF PAYMENT

A supplier will always want terms of payment which are most favourable for him, such as payment with the order. An importer would like payment terms that enable him to make payments after he has sold and secured payment from his customer, ie he would like credit terms such as payment not due for 30, 60, 90, 180 or 360 days from the date of the invoice. It is even more attractive to the importer if he is able to have goods on consignment, ie he doesn't pay the supplier until he has sold the goods to his customers.

Many art galleries take goods from artists and craftsmen only on a consignment sale or return basis. Provided the supplier and the importer agree on the maximum length of time the art gallery can hold the goods on display, eg a work of art, before it is returned to the artist, this is not an unreasonable way of doing business. The artist has his work on display free of charge and gets paid when it is sold or returned to him if it is not sold.

There are many different forms of payment in international trade and anyone intending to become an importer should make themselves familiar with the main types and the terms used to describe them. All the major clearing banks provide free booklets on terms of payment and a copy should be obtained from your local clearing branch or the international trade section of the bank. In any case, contact should be established with the international section staff as sooner or later it will be necessary to discuss with them the various possible forms of payment and any currency exchange problems that may arise, and how to manage them.

The growing use of the Internet to source goods and services means that reasonably assured methods of payment, such as credit card payments, will be required by the suppliers for purchases via the Internet. Buyers should ensure they can recover their payment in the event of non-delivery or the delivery of incorrect or damaged goods.

CASH PAYMENT

The simplest forms of payment from the supplier's viewpoint are cash with order, cash before despatch or cash on delivery, ie COD terms. On COD, the carrier delivering the goods, such as Parcel Force, will only hand over the goods on receipt of payment; many international carriers such as TNT, Federal Express and DHL, in addition to Parcel Force, are quite willing to collect the money for a fee. It is possible for the importer to arrange for his carrier to collect and pay for the goods ex-works from the supplier, in which case the importer is responsible for all charges, insurance and duties. The carrier will normally ensure that all documents are correct regardless of whether he is acting for the importer or the supplier.

OPEN ACCOUNT TRADING

The European single market is becoming more harmonized and it is not unreasonable for a reputable importer to expect to pay for his purchases in the same way as he pays for them in the UK. In any case, suppliers in mainland Europe are likely to be willing to offer the same payment terms as UK suppliers so as to be competitive and provided they are confident the importer is trustworthy and reliable.

The open account trading system simply means that the importer pays the supplier against his invoice. Payment may be cash against invoice or within 30 days or for some other credit period. The importer arranges with his bank for the supplier to be paid by the quickest and cheapest route. Clearing banks now offer a number of different payment routes which vary in speed and cost, and you should decide which route to use after discussions with your bank and your supplier. Payment by ordinary cheque may be an expensive and slow way for the supplier, and a money transfer system may be in his best interest.

The European Commission has been applying pressure on banks throughout the Community to try to persuade them to adopt payment and clearing systems which are as quick and cheap as those in use in their own domestic markets, such as in the UK. This is partly to facilitate the introduction of the single European currency, the 'Euro'. The first group of EU countries will be trading using the Euro in 1999. In the year 2002 at the latest, Euro bank notes and coins will be issued and run parallel with national currencies. Suppliers in single currency countries will expect UK buyers to pay in Euros. Most UK importers are likely to have Euro currency accounts with their own banks. They will be able to issue Euro cheques and transfer Euro payments. The banks have established new settlement systems so suppliers will receive payments into their accounts without delays.

DOCUMENTARY COLLECTIONS

The advantage of the documentary collection system to the importer is that he does not have to make payment for the goods until he accepts the documents relating to them from his own bank. The documents will have been sent by the seller via his own bank to the importer's bank. However, if the importer does not collect the documents he may be faced with penalties.

.The importer's bank receives all the shipping documents and the invoices which state the methods of payment. The bank will notify the importer when it has all the documents. The importer will then pay at sight or accept a term bill of exchange for payment. Provided this method of payment is accepted by his bank, the importer will receive the shipping documents which enable him to obtain the goods. There are various terms used for immediate payment, in addition to 'payment at sight'; these include 'cash against documents', 'documents against payment' and for term bills 'documents against acceptance'. A *term bill* is one that allows credit, ie 30, 60 or 120 days or even longer from date of invoice or date of bill of lading, before payment is made by the importer's bank from the importer's account.

A *bill of exchange* is passed by the exporter's bank to the importer's bank at the time the goods are despatched. A bill of lading, air waybill or similar document must be included with these documents as evidence of despatch. The exporter should arrange with his freight forwarder or with you where the goods will be held awaiting release for when you present the shipping documents. The documents will show the goods are being delivered to a specific place, eg a customs warehouse, to await release. Problems arise where goods are being shipped very quickly by air or road since the goods may arrive before the shipping documents, and the exporter may have to make special arrangements for your bank to have the documents before the goods arrive. Errors and delays in documentary payment arrangements can be a disadvantage, as well as costly, to all parties involved in the transactions. However, increasingly the electronic transfer of documents is being used to increase speed and efficiency. The Simpler Trade Procedures Board (Sitpro) and the Electronic Commerce Association (ECA) are able to give advice and recommendations on electronic systems and their use and acceptability in overseas countries.

LETTERS OF CREDIT (LC)

A documentary LC is a type of payment in which the importer arranges with his own bank for the issue of a letter of credit, ie payment via the importer's and exporter's banks to the exporter, subject to certain conditions. For the exporter to obtain payment, all his shipping and any other documents must comply exactly with the instructions laid down in the letter of credit. Hence, it is important that as an importer you do not lay down onerous conditions that are difficult for the exporter to meet. In addition, you should be willing to agree to any reasonable request for amendments that may be requested by the exporter, such as changes to final shipping dates.

Almost all countries and banks worldwide subscribe to a set of rules known as *uniform customs and practice* (UCP). The latest version of these rules, known as UCP 500, came into operation in January 1994. Although UCP 500 is not legally binding, it will be taken into consideration in any dispute, provided a condition is included in the letter of credit stating that it is subject to UCP 500.

Copies of UCP 500 and related papers can be obtained from your bank or from the International Chamber of Commerce (ICC) office in London. A new version of UCP rules is currently being considered and importers should be alert for their introduction. Blank letters of credit can be obtained from stationery suppliers of international trade forms and sometimes from your own bank. The bank will help you complete them but you must be careful to specify the documents and conditions you require to protect yourself against faulty practices, such as the delivery of wrong or faulty goods, unreal shipping dates and unsuitable payment requirements. Normally, letters of credit are irrevocable, so once opened they cannot be cancelled; however, amendments can be made through the participating banks by agreement between the exporter and yourself. Provided the exporter's documents comply with the letter of credit you will have to pay for the goods regardless of their actual quality and condition on arrival.

To open an LC the importer must make available to his bank the money to cover the LC or arrange for the money to be available when required, especially if he is receiving credit from an exporter. Such credit may be for anything up to 360 days but more usually it is for 30 or 60 days. The cost of this credit is likely to be reflected in the price of the goods.

The exporter may ask for the letter of credit to be confirmed. This means that the bank, normally in the exporter's country, will guarantee payment under the LC once the exporter has fulfilled all terms and conditions in the document. The exporter stipulates the confirming bank in his own country but does not usually pay the confirming fees. However, sometimes the exporter will pay them to ensure that he receives payment if the importer is unwilling to pay for confirmation.

In addition to the normal letters of credit described above, there are special LCs such as standby, revolving and transferable LCs. Smaller importers are unlikely to use any of these unless they purchase regularly from one overseas supplier and wish to use a *revolving* LC to avoid having continuously to open a new LC every time a delivery is required. Your bank will explain how you can open a revolving LC.

The buyer and seller who are the parties to an LC should ensure that they agree the following points to be included in the LC:

- Description of the goods.
- Price and delivery terms.
- Latest date for shipment.
- Method of payment, place of payment, currency.
- Method of shipment, ie air, road, rail or sea.
- With or without transshipment.
- Part shipment allowed or not allowed.
- Documents required by the buyer, eg certificate of origin, guarantee certificate, invoices, import licences etc.
- Responsibility for bank charges and confirmation fees.

Your bank will expect all these points to be included when you open an LC. Furthermore, you will normally require a pro forma invoice to present to your bank as the main proof of your LC requirements. A pro forma invoice is the same as a normal invoice with the words 'pro forma' on it, and is regarded as a sample specimen invoice. The normal invoice is submitted with other documents by the seller to his own bank when he is seeking payment of the LC.

Should the seller receive an LC containing instructions with which he is unable to comply, he should immediately telephone or fax you with the request that you issue instructions to your bank to make an amendment. Provided the bank agrees, it will immediately inform the seller's bank of the amendment. This most frequently arises when there is a delay in the departure of a ship leading to shipment after the final nominated shipping date. Unless the exporter knows you well, he will not ship until he has your amendment giving a new final shipping date, thus leading to further delays. However, if you are confident in each other, he will 'ship on trust,' knowing you will issue an amendment and therefore anticipate it to avoid further delays.

SITPRO issue a letter of credit checklist and guide which is of considerable help to both importers and exporters.

CREDIT

Should the exporter be willing to give you credit there are two ways in which this can happen, depending on whether your payment is by a documentary or a non-documentary system.

The *non-documentary method* is the simplest, and you can arrange it with your supplier as you would in the UK. His invoice will state the final date by which it must be paid, often so many days from the date of invoice or date of shipment, and any penalties you may incur if you are late; similarly, he may give a discount for early payment. There are problems with this type of payment as powerful and to some extent unethical customers deliberately delay payment until after the final date and await demand notes and even the threat of legal action before they pay. If such practices become commonplace, they can become damaging to a country's economy, forcing many small businesses into bankruptcy.

If payment is by the *documentary method*, the normal way of giving and accepting credit is by means of a term *bill of exchange*, described on p 16.

It is fairly common practice within Europe for sellers to ask the buyer's bank to *avalise* bills of exchange. This means that the importer's bank is guaranteeing payment. Should the bill not be avalised and the importer fails to pay the bill on maturity, your supplier may ask your bank to 'protest' the bill as unpaid.

Your bank will instruct a notary public who, in turn, will require you to state the reason for non-payment on a 'deed of protest'. This, together with the dishonoured bill, is the basis for any legal action against you. In the meantime, while the bill remains unpaid, the exporter may have arranged for the return of the goods or for them to be released to someone else, eg to his agent. The exporter will not want his goods held any length of time in a warehouse as he will be incurring additional demurrage (warehousing) and insurance charges. The International Chamber of Commerce issues a code of practice for bank drafts and bills of exchange entitled *Uniform rules for collections* which should be helpful in resolving any problems.

FINANCING YOUR IMPORTS

It is not always easy for a firm to finance its purchases, especially if it has to pay for its imports before they are despatched. One possibility is to seek additional finance from the bank as well as credit from suppliers. There are also a variety of other organizations who will assist small businesses with loans. In every case where you are seeking financial help you will need to produce an up-to-date business plan and be able to demonstrate clearly how and when you expect to repay the loan.

MAKING PAYMENTS

There are a variety of ways in which an importer can remit funds abroad to pay for goods and services, for example:

Cheque

This may appear to be the simplest way since it is the way you would pay in the UK. However, you or your supplier will find yourselves faced with additional bank charges for cross-border payments. These are particularly onerous for small transactions. Your supplier may find there is a considerable delay between the time when he presents your cheque for payment and when the money is credited to his account. This arises particularly when his bank is negotiating your cheque with your bank by post instead of using an electronic transfer system. Unfortunately, some bank transfers can also fail and this causes problems for you and your supplier.

Banker's draft

As the importer you can arrange for your bank to issue a draft drawn in favour of your supplier either in sterling or in a foreign currency. Payment is assured when your supplier presents the draft to his bank. Should you be selling goods yourself in the same foreign currency as you are paying for them it may be advantageous to have an account in this foreign currency either at your local UK bank or in an overseas bank, preferably in a branch or correspondent bank of your bank in the country concerned. This will reduce the costs of currency transactions and the risks associated with fluctuations in exchange rates.

International payment order

A courier or airmail service will be used by your bank to instruct a bank in your supplier's country to pay him. Clearly, your supplier needs to advise you where he wishes to be paid.

International money order

This is an easy way to pay small amounts. Simply ask your bank for a money order and send it to your supplier. Payment is assured when the supplier pays it into his account.

Electronic transfer systems

All the UK banks are developing electronic transfer systems to meet the recommendations of the European Commission. Currently, money is usually sent abroad electronically using SWIFT, the inter-bank electronic network. Fax and telex systems supplement SWIFT when necessary. Your own bank will send funds electronically via SWIFT to its correspondent bank in the country of your supplier. These funds will then be credited to your supplier's account if it is held by the correspondent bank; if not, the latter will send the funds through the local settlement system to your supplier's bank; alternatively, the correspondent bank will contact your supplier to arrange for funds to be collected or paid into an account.

The European Commission concerned with banking has adopted a Directive establishing the essential conditions for long-distance, cross-border payments. It requires banks to:

- observe their contracted commitments with regard to time limits for completing transfers;
- ban double levies;

- reimburse for unsuccessful transfers;
- set transparency conditions for transfers (conditions which are clear to all parties).

This Directive is supported by a communication on the competition rules which the Commission intends to apply to interbank agreements establishing cross-border transfer systems. The Directive should be in force in 1998.

International traders may be surprised to learn that the services provided by the UK are better than anywhere else in Europe and lead the way in meeting the requirements of the European Commission. The development of electronic input methods enables importers to give instruction to their banks to move funds with a minimum of delay using their personal computers and a modem. Euro payments methods available for payments from the UK include:

- chaps Euro – clearing house automated payments system
- Euro 1 – Euro banking association Euro 1 system
- correspondent banking
- bank draft
- BACS–Bacs Ltd automated clearing house system
- international credit cards.

It is important to discuss the type of service you want with your bank in order to decide which is the most convenient and least expensive. Clearly, you will require the account name and number and the bank sorting code at your supplier's bank for this system to be effective; if you make mistakes, they will not be easy to rectify but it should be easier than it has been in the past. Should the correspondent bank or the paying agent be at fault then recourse is possible to recover funds that have been mislaid or paid incorrectly.

CONSIGNMENT STOCKS

An importer is often attracted by the idea that the supplier should provide him with stocks which he holds and only pays for when he has sold them. When to pay for the stocks, how to keep and check records and when physically to check stocks still held can often cause problems.

The supplier would naturally like to be paid as soon as you invoice for any stock sold to your customers, whereas you would prefer not to pay for this stock until you have received the money from your customer. It is essential for the importer and his supplier to be quite clear when the importer pays. If the importer pays on a monthly basis for goods invoiced or sold to his customers, this can lead to problems in reconciling sales with remaining stocks. Unless there is very good management of stocks held, stocks sold and stocks received, and the oldest stock is always sold first, disputes are likely to arise particularly over the original value of stock sold.

A problem can also arise in relation to improved products becoming available before old stocks are sold: should the old stock be retained or sold off at a discount, and who pays for any loss or costs involved? There are many risks attached to consignment stock trading which can only lead to payment disputes unless there is very good management and understanding by both parties.

4

Sales Conditions and Agreements

All importers will find that suppliers have standard terms and conditions of sale. In addition, if they are to act as a manufacturer's official agent or distributor they will need to enter into an agreement with them. These agreements are increasingly subject to legal requirements within the European Union and importers should have them checked out by a commercial lawyer before agreeing to them.

SALES CONDITIONS

It is a seller's normal practice to have a standard set of sales terms and conditions which are printed on the back of his quotation forms. They may also be printed on the back of his invoices or attached to them.   Similarly, they should be attached to any sale contract. Any quotation should state on the front of the document that the terms and conditions are attached so that they will then form part of the sales contract should you place an order. Your supplier should also refer to these terms and conditions when acknowledging an order. A number of trade associations provide information on terms and conditions for their industries.   If this is not available, a commercial lawyer should be able to provide you with a set which is applicable to your industry, although you may only wish him to check those used by your suppliers. This is especially important if you intend to enter into a formal agency or distribution agreement.

The following are typical subjects which you should expect to see included in terms and conditions of sale:

- Price: Duration and variability
- Quantity: Tolerances

- Quality: Fitness for what purpose and specifications
- Warranties: Guarantees
- Liabilities: Liability limitation, time limit on claims
- Delivery: Any special conditions or requirements
- Packaging: Any special provisions
- Payment: Interest on overdue accounts
- Default of buyer: Right to cancel the contract
- Risk and property: When risk passes from seller to buyer
- Force majeure: Strikes, wars and government interference
- Arrangement: Seller's right to sell – contraction or
                      assignment of benefits
- Insurance: Any special needs
- Incoterms: Statement that Incoterms apply (see p 32)
- Diversions of goods: Seller's right to divert
- Arbitration: Who will arbitrate in disputes
- Law: Specification that European Union and
                      English Law apply
- Jurisdiction: Specification of UK arbitration or English
                      Courts

It is important to remember that if you are acting as an agent, distributor or stockist and reselling the imported goods, you must apply the same set of terms and conditions to your customers.

ORDERS

The order and confirmation of the receipt of an order should include certain essential information to avoid any misunderstanding. For example:

- names and addresses of buyer and seller (ie importer and exporter);
- VAT numbers for buyer and seller if both situated within the EU;
- product details including package information;
- method of transport;
- payment and delivery terms;
- value of the order including any agreed charges;
- delivery promise or indication;
- any other details required.

Naturally, both buyer and seller should discuss their purchasing conditions and sales terms and conditions respectively, if only to confirm to each other that they are the standard terms and conditions used in their industry and to agree them. Should either party to the transaction be using any terms or conditions that are not standard, they should draw them to the attention of the other party.

AGREEMENTS

The importer may find it desirable to enter into formal agreements with his suppliers to be a selling agent and distributor. In fact, some suppliers may insist on a formal agreement before they will allow the importer to sell or stock their products. Formal agreements help to protect both parties against unfair competition and to define how they will work together. The new agency regulations provide that either party may demand a written agreement or memorandum of terms and conditions of any oral agreement.

Any importer entering into a formal agreement should ensure that none of the terms is contrary to the requirements of EU directives and regulations on, for example, competition, health and safety and the new agency law. The latter applies only to agents and not to distributors, who buy and sell goods. An agent may be an individual, a company or a partnership who acts as a self-employed intermediary. The agency law applies only to those agents who have ongoing authority to negotiate and sometimes to conclude the sale or purchase of goods on behalf of the supplier, ie the principal. It does not apply to the sale and purchase of services. Information on the EU agency law and regulations can be found in the HMSO publication Statutory Instrument No 3035 (1993) 'The Commercial Agents (Council Directive) Regulations 1993'. These agency regulations imply mandatory terms in regulated agreements.

Agency and distribution agreements can easily fall foul of UK and EU laws and regulations; in addition, while some clauses appear in most agreements there may be others which are special to an agreement. It is for this reason, and to ensure an agreement is legally correct, that you should always have agreements checked by a lawyer for international trade. Never sign an agreement submitted to you by your supplier or send him one composed by yourself until it has been approved and, where necessary, amended by a suitably experienced lawyer.

In order to draw up a draft agreement for your supplier–importer relationship, simply obtain copies of existing agreements or refer to a suitable one in a relevant publication and modify it to meet your needs. Then submit your draft agreement to your lawyer. Alternatively, list the commercial points you wish to include in the agreement and ask your lawyer to draft it. The latter is usually preferable and is likely to be cheaper if you are clear what points you want included.

AGENCY AGREEMENTS

There are certain essential clauses for inclusion in an agency agreement and a sample agreement is given in Chapter 12. Many of these clauses may also appear in a distribution agreement. The main agency agreement clauses are explained below.

The parties. This states who are the parties to the agreement and where they each have their principal place of business. They should be identified clearly.

Purpose. This deals with the appointment of the agent, which may be non-exclusive, sole (ie principal can still sell direct) or exclusive (principal cannot deal direct).

Goods. Usually, this describes in general terms the product to be sold by the agent. If desirable, a list of the products may be included in an attached schedule with a proviso that the principal may amend the list at any time subject to a period of notice, eg one month.

Territory. A description of the territory, eg region or country for which the agent is responsible.

Principal's duties. In this clause the principal may agree to advise the agent of any enquiries, orders and any other queries received direct from customers in the agent's territory. The principal may also agree to provide samples and literature for new products free of charge.

Agent's duties. Usually, this requires the agent to use his best endeavours to sell the products to customers of sound commercial standing and to advise the principal of his sales progress. He may also be required to notify the principal of any regulations that may affect the import and sale of the products. (If the agent is to be a sole agent, this must be stated.) The agent may also be required not to sell, supply or manufacture competing goods except with the written agreement of the principal.

Exceptions and inclusions. Certain customers who insist on dealing through their overseas buying agent directly with the principal at his head office might be excluded from the agreement. The agent may be allowed to appoint sub-agents.

Quotation. This refers to the price of the products, usually listed in an attached price schedule. The clause should state that the principal may change his prices subject to a period of notice, eg three months.

Stock. If the agent is to hold stocks of samples, this should be stated. The samples up to a certain quantity per annum may be required to be supplied free of charge; the agent may also be required to hold emergency stocks and spare parts. These are normally bought by the agent for resale. How any emergency stock and spare parts will be priced to the agent should also be stated.

Communication, travel costs. Normally, a principal and an agent should pay their own communication and travel costs. This should apply when they visit each other and when the principal visits customers in the market. The agent may be required to visit the principal every other year and the principal to visit the agent and some of the customers every alternate year.

Alternative suppliers. This may allow the agent to purchase and resell similar goods from another supplier in a situation in which the principal is unable to supply goods and the buyer's requirements must be satisfied because, for example, his production might otherwise be stopped (see Agent's duties).

Commission. The terms under which an agent will be paid his commission, eg within 30 days of the principal receiving payments, should be stated. The rates of commission are usually set out in an attached schedule.

Records. The agent should be required to keep sales records and accounts relating to the sale of the principal's products for inspection by the principal. The principal should supply the agent with monthly statements of commission due and the agent should have the right to be provided with information, eg copies of sales invoices, to enable him to check the commission due.

Promotion. This should set out the ways in which the agent is expected to promote the sales of the product. It should not only include the use of sales representatives but possibly also advertising, promotional articles, direct mail and taking stands at certain exhibitions. The principal should state the extent to which he is willing to assist with the promotion financially, with his own staff and with promotional literature.

Reports. The sole agent should be required to submit regular sales and market reports and the principal should regularly supply information on his products and product developments.

Trade marks and patents. Usually the agent is required to assist with the protection of trade marks and patents.

Force majeure. This frees the principal from any responsibilities for late delivery or failure to deliver due to unforeseen causes, eg fire, war, tempest. The principal should agree to inform the agent promptly of any such failure and to provide a certificate where necessary.

Breach of agreement. In the event of either party failing to abide by the agreement, the other party shall have the right to summarily cancel the agreement in writing.

Duration and termination. The initial period of the agreement, eg one year, the renewal of terms, eg automatically renewed for the next year unless three months' notice of termination is given before the end of the year, should be stated. The terms of termination, if not covered by the renewal terms, should also be given. This may be three months' notice given by either party. Under European Union regulations it will also be necessary to include compensation terms.

Law and arbitration. This normally states that the agreement is subject to the laws of England and that in the event of a dispute which cannot be settled by the parties, it shall be referred to arbitration in the UK or the courts of England and Wales, or to the International Court of Arbitration.

DISTRIBUTION AGREEMENTS

The agreements often include clauses relating to the minimum amount of stock of each product the distributors shall hold. The principal may also agree to finance the agent's stock by special credit terms or even by agreeing to consignment stocks. These are stocks for which the agent pays when he has sold them. Consignment transactions are often difficult to monitor and lead to arguments between agents and principals (see p 21).

Importers may also take goods on a sale or return basis, which is a form of consignment business. This system is very common among art galleries who take artists' work on a sale or return basis.

In many countries, it is not possible for the principal to stipulate to a distributor the price at which a product will be sold. Resale price maintenance for most products was abolished in the UK some years ago. In the UK it is still possible to be a sole importer of products from a specific supplier which may give him a near monopoly. However, he is still subject to the competition laws in the European Union and in the UK.

In general, the clauses in a distribution agreement will be similar to those in an agency agreement, taking into account some of the points mentioned below. A sample distribution agreement is included in Chapter 12. However, some of the following comments may be helpful:

DISTRIBUTION AGREEMENT CLAUSES

The parties
This should give the registered names, addresses and VAT numbers of the parties to the agreement.

Definition
It is important to define any terms used in the agreement and in the associated schedules.

Purpose
This deals with the appointment of the distributor and the territory and products for which he will be responsible.

Distributor's duties

These need to be described in some detail if conflicts are to be avoided.

Principal's duties

These may be covered under a 'Supply of Products' clause and concern the terms and conditions under which he will supply the distributor and matters concerning prices and product changes.

Stock

The principal may require the distributor to hold minimum stocks for each product and reorder in minimum quantities. This is particularly important when the distributor is responsible for supplying spare parts and providing an after-sales service.

Protection of patents, trademarks and copyright

This limits the distributor's use of intellectual property rights. It also requires him to report any infringements in his territory and to assist the principal to defend his rights. A clause may also be included to protect confidential information on the principal's products and business.

Duration and termination

This covers not only the rights of either parties to terminate the agreement according to certain conditions but the right of the distributor to compensation when it is terminated.

SALE-OR-RETURN AGREEMENT

Reference has been made to a type of agreement which is commonly used between gallery shops, eg artwork shops and artists and designer-craftsmen. Those retailers handling works from artists and craftsmen, situated abroad but most probably in European markets, should ensure that they have clearly written agreements.

The Crafts Council in London has a short guide (quoted below with the Council's permission) to assist interested parties to formulate a suitable agreement which has some similarity with the agreements already discussed. Clauses in this agreement should include:

Parties to the agreement. The names, addresses, telephone numbers and VAT numbers of the gallery and the artist.

List of works. This should detail the articles to be supplied, the retail price, the commission to the gallery and whether or not the prices include VAT. It should state how long the gallery will retain each work, the numbers sold at the end of each period and when those unsold should be returned.

Ownership. This states that the articles remain the property of the artist until he has received payment in full.

Payment. This states how and when the artist will be informed of and paid for sales. In addition, the artist may require to be given the names and addresses of all purchasers. The gallery should use an agreed contract of sale.

Copyright. The artist retains copyright in the work.

Insurance. The gallery is required to maintain the article adequately and have insurance against any loss, damage and theft and to repair any damage.

Reproduction. Limitation on the gallery's use of reproductions, eg postcards and posters and how they may be used by the gallery.

The terms and conditions should be agreed and signed by both parties.

PURCHASING CONDITIONS

Many larger companies and some smaller ones have standard conditions of purchase which are designed to help the importer to maintain purchasing standards and potential suppliers to meet his requirements. The terms and conditions are normally printed on the back of the purchaser's enquiry and order forms, and references made to them on the front.

The terms and conditions contain clauses which define their purpose, scope and duration. A clause may state the importer's purchasing policy in respect of matters such as prices and payment, eg that they must be in pounds sterling. It may also include a statement on the importer's obligations to the supplier and vice versa. It may state for how long the enquiry or order is valid, eg two months, from the date on the form. A clause may cover operational procedures and jurisdiction. The need for all goods to meet the importer's buying specification will probably be included. Other clauses may also be included, eg on confidentiality. Advice on what clauses to be included may be obtained from the Chartered Institute of Purchasing and Supply although it will be necessary to become a member to obtain their full services.

Purchasing conditions, or more specifically, contract conditions, become even more important when an importer wishes to enter into a long-term contract arrangement with a supplier. Such a contract would have to include clauses covering termination, waiver, force majeure, assignment, jurisdiction and responsibility for missing and damaged goods, or any failures to meet specification. In drawing up such contract terms it is important to seek the advice and assistance of experienced commercial lawyers.

5

Transporting the Product

DELIVERING PARCELS AND DOCUMENTS

The simplest way for suppliers to send parcels and documents to importers is by national rail and parcel services, private express parcel carriers such as Federal Express, TNT and DHL, and by courier. Express freight services have become an established part of the transport system in Europe and North America. Usually the goods are guaranteed to be delivered within 24 or 48 hours of despatch. The freight costs can be quite high but most companies will quote lower rates for longer delivery times. Naturally, express freight services are more costly than those provided by the traditional national mail services such as the Royal Mail and Parcel Force, although they also offer express delivery services. Most of the express service companies also offer a documentation and payment collection service so your supplier can deal directly with them, instead of using a freight forwarder.

It is important to discuss with your supplier what level of delivery service you require since there can be significant differences in cost between the various levels. The normal mail service for post and parcel is usually the cheapest but the delivery times may be unacceptable. You should also remember that ordinary mail and express services have limitations on the size and weight of package they will carry; usually the maximum weight is 15 kilos.

MOVING BULK PRODUCTS

The successful movement of goods is vital to both importers and exporters. Attention to detail is most important when planning to move goods from one country to another. Most importers prefer to have goods delivered either to their own warehouse or to some other point where they can arrange for the goods to be picked up by their own inland transport. However, some companies prefer to buy from a customer on an ex-works basis, arranging for a carrier to collect the goods for them.

There are many organizations engaged in freight forwarding, clearing and transporting who are available to assist an importer. One of the first points of contact to find a suitable organization should be the British International Freight Association (BIFA) which works also with the Institute of Freight Forwarders. They will supply you with a list of members who can arrange the documentation and movement of goods from your supplier overseas or a clearing agent who will arrange the clearance of your goods through a UK port and deliver to your warehouse.

It is important to tell BIFA the type of goods you wish to move and the countries where they are to be collected, and they will suggest members who have the right knowledge and experience to act for you. Importers must understand all aspects of moving goods so they can discuss modes of transport, delivery terms, packaging, labelling and documentation with their supplier and freight forwarder.

DELIVERY TERMS

A key part in any price quotations are the delivery terms. They can affect prices and the importer's own costs quite significantly. All importers should be aware of the meaning of delivery terms, their use and which obligations relate to the importer and which to the supplier.

Delivery terms have been incorporated into a generally accepted international code by the International Chamber of Commerce (ICC) under the title 'Incoterms'. The order of the terms in this code are EXW, FCA, FOB, CFR, CIF, CPT, CIP, DAF, DES, DEQ, DDU/DPP. A booklet giving detailed information on all these terms can be obtained direct from the ICC in London although it may also be available from your local Chamber of Commerce. The main terms in use have the following meanings.

Ex-works (EXW)

The importer arranges for the collection of the goods from the seller's premises and acquires title to the goods at the time of loading. Normally, the cost of packaging and labelling the goods ready for collection and transport is the responsibility of the seller but any additional packaging will be up to the buyer. Transport, insurance and associated costs are the responsibility of the buyer. The insurance should cover possible damage or loss from where goods are loaded as well as during loading.

Free carrier (FCA)

This term is used instead of FOB when through road transport is used and includes roll on and roll off (ro/ro) ferries. It is also used for container shipments where different types of transport are used on a door-to-door basis instead of port to port. The goods pass to the buyer at the time and place (destination) stated in the sales contract. This may be an inland depot. The seller must notify the buyer, by means of a quick communication, when the goods are to be handed over to the carrier in accordance with instructions from the buyer. Up to the point where the carrier receives them the seller has the title and risk in the goods; after that the buyer has the title and risk.

Free on board (FOB)

The seller is responsible for packing, labelling and delivering the goods on board a vessel at the port stipulated by the buyer. The latter may also stipulate the line or vessel to be used. The seller is responsible for all costs and risks until the goods have passed over the ship's rail, and he must advise the buyer of all shipping information when the goods are on board.

Cost and freight (CFR)

The seller is responsible for all costs including packaging and labelling up to the point where the goods are loaded on board a ship plus the cost of freight to the agreed point of discharge. The seller insures the goods until they are loaded, whereat the importer becomes responsible for all risks. The exporter is responsible for any export licences and the importer for any import licences. The goods must be despatched in the period stipulated in the sales contract. The exporter must obtain a clear, negotiable bill of lading and pass it to the buyer or his bank via his own bank.

Cost, insurance and freight (CIF)

The obligations are much the same as under CFR but the exporter is responsible for the insurance policy that covers risk in transit to the named point of destination, usually the agreed port of discharge. This insurance policy should be for the CIF price plus 10 per cent to cover the costs of goods if they have to be returned. The importer should insist on an 'all risk' type of insurance policy which, if possible, should be in the same currency as the sales contract.

Freight carriage paid (CPT)

This is common in Europe when road transport or multi-modal transport is used. The exporter obtains any necessary licences and arranges and pays transport to the destination point. The exporter is responsible for all risks to the goods until the first carrier physically receives them, when the risks pass to the importer. The latter is responsible for import licences and customs duties. The exporter must notify the importer by rapid communication, eg fax, as soon as he has passed the goods to the first carrier.

Freight carriage and insurance paid (CIP)

This is the same as CPT except the exporter must take out cargo insurance to cover up to the agreed delivery point. The importer is also entitled to claim under the exporter's insurance policy and he must be advised by the exporter of the nature and extent of cover of the insurance policy.

Delivery duty unpaid (DDU) or delivery duty paid (DDP)

The price to the exporter covers all delivery costs to the importer's premises with any import duties being paid by the importer if it is DDU or by the seller if it is DDP. Any mode of transport can be stipulated. The exporter must advise the buyer as soon as the goods are received by the first carrier. The benefit to the importer of DDP is that he knows accurately the price for the goods and so can calculate his own cost and profit margins with confidence.

Other Incoterms are used less often and are as follows:

Free alongside ship (FAS)

The exporter delivers the goods alongside the ship, eg on to the quay or to the warehouse to await loading. The buyer must arrange shipment including payment and clearance for export, export and import duties, loading, transport, insurance and import clearance.

Delivered at frontier (DAF)

This is used for road and multi-modal transport. The seller is responsible for the goods until they reach the frontier of the country of destination.

Delivered ex-ship (DES)

The seller is responsible for the goods until they are unloaded at the destination port.

Delivered ex-quay (DEQ)

The seller is responsible for the goods until they leave the quay at the port of destination, and hence the seller may be responsible for customs clearance.

Ex-ship (EXS)

The exporter is responsible for the goods until they are unloaded at the stipulated destination port.

Ex-quay (EXQ)

The seller is responsible for the goods until they leave the quay at the point of destination. He may be responsible for customs clearance.

It is most important that importers understand delivery terms and the nature of their obligations and those of the seller. The importer should be prepared to negotiate delivery terms with the seller as part of the price. A typical seller's quotation might be: 'Product name' £10 per kilo FOB 'departure port'.

TRANSPORT MODE

There are several different modes of transport and often a variety of carriers. These modes include road, rail, sea and air, and any freight movement may involve the use of more than one mode. A professional guide is published each year by the Institute of Freight Forwarders (IFF) called 'The Exporter and Forwarder'. Handling freight and all the associated documentation, especially outside the European Union, can be complicated. Many carriers will now carry out the work of freight forwarders and clearers so importers should shop around for the help they need. They will find it useful to contact the IFF to obtain a list of the firms that can provide them with appropriate assistance. When contacting the Institute they should state the nature of the goods to be carried, from which country or countries they will be arriving and for which costs, etc relating to the transport of goods, they think they will be responsible.

An importer needs to acquire an understanding of the transport market, the modes of transport and the services available, including the cost difference between one service and another. Transport costs can seriously affect an importer's costs. He should look around for the mode of transport, speed of delivery, reliability and overall costs that best meet his needs.

INTERNATIONAL ROAD HAULAGE

Road transport to and from the UK with Continental Europe, the Middle East and North Africa is increasing with the use of the Channel Tunnel. The ro/ro ferries between Europe and Africa and other destinations have also enabled sea crossings to be undertaken without any serious hold-ups.

There are two means of international haulage – driver-accompanied operations and unaccompanied ones. In the former the driver, possibly with another driver, accompanies the vehicle from its point of loading to its point of unloading. Some long-distance lorries contain sleeping accommodation and other facilities for the drivers, so one driver can drive while the other sleeps; on other vehicles the driver will stop in specially guarded vehicle parks while he rests or sleeps.

The unaccompanied service usually involves a tractor and trailer. The trailer is hauled by the tractor to the loading point of shipment. It then leaves the place of departure unaccompanied by the tractor and driver, and a new tractor and driver collect the trailer at its unloading point. The trailer is thus in the charge of port and shipping employees once it has been separated from its tractor.

. Unaccompanied services are generally cheaper than accompanied services as there is no tractor to take up shipping space and no driver to transport. However, the goods may suffer damage during movement between transport modes and there is a greater risk of pilferage. It is therefore most important to select a reliable service if the goods are to be shipped in unaccompanied trailers.

INTERNATIONAL RAIL HAULAGE

The development of the Channel Tunnel rail service has opened up Europe and the UK to much faster freight and parcel traffic. There are seven UK terminals for freight at Willesden, Birmingham, Manchester, Cardiff, Mossend, Middlesbrough and the port of Liverpool connected with up to 18 terminals on mainland Europe. Manchester is within 35 hours by rail of Milan. Railfreight Distribution is responsible for the UK's international freight strategy and this includes the operation of frequent long-distance trains via the Channel Tunnel to and from the UK terminals. The terminals in the UK and on the Continent act as hubs, and include Paris, Milan, Madrid, Barcelona, Valencia, Basle, Vienna, Muizen and Duisburg. Railfreight Distribution has three intermodal transport operators: Combined Transport Ltd (CTL), Allied Continental Intermodal (ACI) and Unilog NV. With their Continental counterparts these intermodal operators buy train services and sell individual container space to transport companies. The latter provide a door-to-door service for their final customer, normally a manufacturer or shipper.

Essentially, intermodal operations consist of combining relatively small consignments of freight into viable trainload quantities for haul through the Tunnel. At UK hub centres, and possibly other centres, there will be local connections by road for the delivery and collection of goods. The same facilities are available at Continental centres. Information on these services can be obtained from Railfreight Distribution. Suppliers in Europe are increasingly using those facilities.

The rail parcel service is operated by Red Star Express Parcels. This service is linked with Red Star Europe and the Eurorail Express System. The Red Star Europe Eurorail parcel point at stations can be used for the delivery and collection of parcels for their quickest movement. Alternatively, the final delivery and collection of parcels can be arranged by road. Importers should discuss with their suppliers and their freight forwarders/clearing agents whether to use road, rail or air transport direct or to leave the choice to their express parcel service or to the exporter's parcel service.

SHIPPING

The most likely use of shipping by small companies is when their products will be travelling with other companies' products in an LCL, ie less than full container load, which implies that it is not a full container load of one manufacturer's products. Small manufacturers who ship bulky goods such as furniture or plastic products that sell in large quantities will probably be shipping in an FCL ('full container load' of one manufacturer's goods).

An LCL container packed with several suppliers' products is usually assembled and packed at a freight carrier's depot in the exporting country and unpacked at the clearing agent's depot in the importing country. This groupage operation leads to an increased risk of losing goods through theft and damage especially in certain badly policed and managed countries. However, if your supplier in one of these countries takes sufficient care and uses reputable companies for the transport of the goods, they should reach the UK without loss or damage.

There is no doubt that the use of containers leads to improved security and faster ship turnaround at the ports. You should distinguish between ferry services such as those between the UK and other European countries, and international routes to deep sea markets beyond Europe. There are many ferry services around Europe, for example in the Baltic and the Mediterranean. These ferries frequently transport lorries or trailers with their tractors which carry sealed containers. In contrast, container ships generally carry the containers only from port to port where they are transshipped to smaller container vessels for other ports or on to lorries for delivery. Importers should be aware how their imports are being shipped to the UK since this will affect their speed of delivery.

AIR FREIGHT

Air freight plays an important part in the movement of goods to the UK, especially for perishable goods such as flowers and soft fruit as well as for light, compact, high value goods. Spare parts which are required urgently may be transported by air. A large number of air freight movements occur each day in and out of the UK. If you are responsible for arranging the transport of your imports to the UK, using the services of a freight forwarder, then both of you should be aware of air freight opportunities. Rates will probably be low for journeys to the UK when there is much more freight going from the UK to your despatch airport.

It should also be remembered that if goods can reach you quickly from distant destinations, you may make a saving on your stock levels which will offset the higher cost of air freight compared with, for example, sea freight. Not only does air freight reduce transit times but it also reduces the time taken for you to obtain replenishment stocks, especially if your supplier holds them. If you are paying for goods on despatch or before they are despatched, you should be able to reduce the time between paying for the goods and when you have them for sale and, in turn, are paid for them; alternatively, you may be able to offer your customers longer credit. Just-in-time supply systems can sometimes mean that your goods will arrive by air rather than by more traditional forms of transport in order to meet delivery times.

Another type of express service is provided by courier companies who arrange for high value goods or important documents to be taken by hand so that they reach their destination within a certain time. Not only can such services provide rapid transportation, using passenger airlines, but couriers can deliver directly to a named person and bring back signed or new documents. The service for documents has declined with the advent of electronic data interchange (EDI), fax and other electronic systems for communicating information and documents, and will continue to do so.

INSURANCE

Importers should be aware from their supplier's payment and delivery terms of the point in a transaction at which they will be responsible for the loss or damage of goods in transit. An importer may acquire title to goods and hence be responsible for their insurance long before he has them on his premises and is able to inspect them physically.

Insurance is a vital part of any international transaction involving the movement of something of value. Importers should use a registered insurance broker experienced in international trade to ensure that they have adequate cover. Freight forwarders and clearing agents who are trading members of the British International Freight Association are able to advise companies on the insurance needed. These freight forwarders and clearers must also have appropriate and sufficient insurance cover for their staff and the services they provide.

CARGO INSURANCE

Cargo insurance is essential for an importer who is buying ex-works or on such terms as FOB or any other terms where he is responsible for insurance during shipment. Insurance must start from the point at which responsibility and usually the title passes from the supplier to the importer. A *certificate of insurance* is a necessary part of shipping documents and should normally be for the value of the goods plus 10 per cent to allow for any additional costs that may be involved in the rejection and/or return of the goods.

A *marine insurance policy* is generally taken out to cover all shipments for which the importer is responsible. It can be extended to cover all modes of transport, reasonable periods of storage, and specific risks such as those due to extreme cold or heat. A *floating or open policy* is one that enables the importer simply to advise his insurance company or broker of each shipment. It is most important that all shipment details, and any other information given under the requirements of the policy, be strictly and correctly provided. Inaccuracies can lead to difficulties with claims. Normally, claims for less than £1000 will be settled without an investigation but for larger claims an independent loss adjuster will be appointed. His task is to make recommendations for the settlement of the claim.

Marine insurance is written in accordance with the Marine Insurance Act 1906, and subsequent changes. Cargo insurance is usually written using the marine all risks (MAR) policy containing three sections of clauses. Section A clauses provide comprehensive cover with certain exclusions while sections B and C clauses give only limited cover. It is essential to discuss with your insurance broker which clauses you wish to be included.

IMPORTING RISKS

An importer faces two main risks when importing. The first concerns the recovery of his money if he has already paid and the goods are faulty, and the second is the foreign exchange risk if he is not paying in sterling. If he pays in sterling, he has no exchange problems but may have to face price changes if sterling moves in value significantly against the currency of his supplier. Should he be paying in a foreign currency, he can protect his own sterling price by buying the foreign currency forward so that it is available when payment falls due or he can make a cash purchase and put the foreign currency on deposit with his bank until it is required.

His bank can also offer other alternatives to protect against currency fluctuations. For example, the importer can take out options to buy the foreign currency at a certain time. This will protect him against adverse exchange rate movements since he can either take up his option at that time or let it lapse, in which case he loses his option fees. It is essential to discuss possible strategies with the international division staff of a bank.

Importers can protect themselves against the delivery of faulty goods by insurance usually for the value of the goods plus at least 10 per cent. If the goods do not arrive or are badly damaged, they can make a claim under their insurance policy to recover their money, assuming they have already paid or are committed to pay. In any event, as soon as an importer is aware that goods are damaged he must call in a loss adjuster to survey the damage.

Importers can also protect themselves by having goods inspected for quality and quantity before they are despatched. Organizations such as SGS Inspection Services Ltd provide services in overseas countries to carry out inspections and to issue certificates. Smaller companies may appoint a local individual to look after their interests and inspect goods before they are despatched. This is a fairly common practice in developing countries where some suppliers, especially new ones, fail to realise how important it is that a whole consignment should be up to standard, the quantity correct, and packaging and labelling in accordance with specifications and international standards.

PRODUCT LIABILITY

Product liability is an increasing problem in the UK and the EU. Importers are likely to find themselves as the first target for any legal actions for product liability. It is therefore important to ensure that such liability is in turn made the responsibility of the supplier or manufacturer through the sales contract or other agreements. Importers should also give consideration to taking out product liability insurance in case they have difficulty recovering any damages or costs from their supplier. It is important to discuss, with an insurance broker, what type of policy is required for your particular type of business.

PACKAGING AND LABELLING – PRESENTATION

Importers must take care to ensure that their suppliers correctly package and label any goods so that they are delivered without any problems arising from package failures or misleading labelling. Packages must be able to protect a product from external damage, mishandling and the weather, eg rain, frost and heat. The package must also be capable of being lifted, stacked or moved either with other packages or alone. It may have to withstand being fork-lifted on a pallet, hoisted on a ship or manhandled. The Institute of Packaging gives advice on packaging and information on package design. In many cases importers may wish to agree a package specification with their supplier and in some instances include it as part of their purchasing conditions.

The movement of the transporting vehicle can subject a package to vibration and sharp swings. Packages may also be manhandled very roughly on their journey to the UK, especially where road and lifting facilities are very poor. In parts of Asia, Africa and South America a package can be subject to much rougher handling than would be the case in Europe.

Packaging can seriously affect the cost so it is important to check with your supplier that he does not use unnecessarily expensive packaging materials and that the package, while being secure, can be assembled and opened reasonably quickly. Packages must also conform to any weight and size limits imposed by carriers. These factors can also affect freight charges. While an outer package has a utilitarian purpose, individual product packages should be made attractive according to the needs of the market. Packages, especially outer packaging, should help to limit pilfering attempts. Finally, a package may be required to have a resale value or be suitable for recycling. In any case, it is important to be aware of any UK or EU environmental regulations that may affect not only the product you import but also its packaging.

Labelling on packages must answer transport needs, in accordance with internationally accepted codes and regulations, as well as any specific regulations that may apply in the UK. Information on UK regulations can be obtained from appropriate government departments. Your trade association should also be able to advise you on these matters. There are specific requirements for such products as dangerous goods, processed foods and pharmaceuticals.

Labelling of the external overall package of your goods should be clear but not so as to attract thieves. Individually packaged items have to be correctly labelled in accordance with UK regulations. Instructions in the use of the product may also have to be on a printed label for each item.

Finally, each individually packaged product must look attractive to potential customers and helpful to potential users. Some packages need to have tops which are difficult for children but not for adults to open, and opening instructions should be included. Labelling and packaging should always be discussed with the supplier even if it is your intention to repack the product for your customers.

6

Import Procedures

All importers need to develop systematic import procedures. This requires a proper understanding of all the documents involved in the import process, knowledge of the roles of the organizations with whom they will be dealing, and how to overcome any problems. The banks, freight forwarders, carriers and Customs and Excise are the bodies with whom they are most likely to be in contact.

The supplier, ie the exporter, will always be responsible for producing certain documents such as the invoice. However, the number of different documents the exporter has to produce will depend upon the type of products he is selling, the country in which he is situated and its trade regulations, and whether or not he is selling ex-works or delivered to the importer's premises. The exporter is responsible for seeing that all the documents he has to produce are complete and accurate. He must also process them speedily and correctly in accordance with his own sales contract and the importer's purchasing conditions.

ORDER PROCESSING

The importer must ensure that all the documents he has to produce, such as enquiry and order forms, specifications, import licences and payment documents, such as letters of credit, are accurate, or unnecessary delays and in turn damage or loss of goods could result.

The efficient processing of orders is vital to the successful operation of the import unit. The following sequence of activities gives an indication of what may be required.

1. Enquiry sent to overseas supplier requesting quotation, delivery schedule, delivery and payment terms, specifications for product packaging and labelling, and purchasing conditions.
2. Acknowledgement of overseas supplier's quotation and request for any amendments. All details of overseas supplier to be recorded. Order placed containing details of your bank, clearing

    agent, VAT number, order number, and letter of credit if neces-
sary. Order in progress chart commenced. Supplier's acknowledgement of order with any amendments to be noted and filed.

3.   If the overseas supplier has UK representatives or agents, their
address, etc should be on file. They should have received a copy
of the order and the acknowledgement from their principal so,
as buyer, you can discuss the order and its progress with them if
necessary.

4.   Check delivery and payment terms and establish that any import
controls will be met, eg that you have the appropriate import
licences. Check that you have made arrangements with your
bank for payment and that your clearing agent is aware of the
order and your payment arrangements. If payment is by documentary collection, your goods cannot be collected until you
have obtained the shipping documents.

5.   If you are buying ex-works, it is most important that you liaise
closely with your freight forwarder or carrier on all the documentation, and for the collection and transport of your goods from
your supplier's works to your premises.

6.   It is important to keep your sales or production department informed of the progress of the order and to advise them as soon
as the goods are received at your premises.

7.   Records should be made of any transit delays and any goods
damaged. Any insurance claims should be put in hand immediately so that an insurance assessor can inspect the goods quickly
if necessary.

CUSTOMS PRACTICE

The Customs and Excise procedures are often the most difficult to
understand for those new to international trade. It is important for
importers to know how to operate them and to keep up to date with
changes in regulations and procedures.

    Customs departments all over the world control the flow of
goods in and out of their country; they collect taxes and duties and
record the movement of goods for various government departments. Clearing goods through UK customs is a complex matter
unless they are on free circulation within the EU. Should you be
importing goods from outside the EU it is generally wisest to
employ a clearing agent if you are responsible for clearing the
goods through customs and for the payment of any duties. The
British International Freight Association (BIFA) will provide names
of company members who act as clearing agents. Should you be
purchasing ex-works from a supplier, BIFA are also able to help you
by providing names of freight forwarders who will arrange transport, handle all the shipping documentation and deal with customs.

HM Customs and Excise have a number of Advice Centres through-out the UK (see Chapter 12). At these centres you can obtain informa-tion and advice on all aspects of your proposed import business in relation to Customs and Excise, as well as a large number of public notices, ie booklets, that are supplied free of charge. Make sure you obtain all the notices relevant to your business by looking at the list of notices and identifying with the Advice Centre those which relate to your activities.

The importer or his representative bringing goods into the UK from outside the Community has to present a customs entry form to the Customs and Excise unit at the place of discharge. This is copy num-ber 6 of the single administrative document (SAD) set. As importer, you will also have a customs procedure code (CPC) number which shows where the goods have come from and whether they are for UK use, for re-export or for further processing. It may also be necessary to attach other documents to the customs entry form such as a form for goods liable for *ad valorem* duty, ie duty based on the value of the goods, plus some documents that should be provided by your sup-plier such as a number of copies of the original invoice. It is impor-tant to ensure that all the necessary information and documents are presented to customs to enable the goods to be cleared. This will help to ensure that you do not overpay duties. Should this happen, you can obtain a refund by means of an inventory certificate. If you underpay, you will have to complete a post-entry certificate obtain-able from Customs and Excise, pay the additional duty and possibly a penalty!

Detailed information on all documents used in the import process from supplier to buyer can be obtained from SITPRO and BIFA. Blank forms can be obtained from the stationery suppliers who specialize in forms required for international trade. All importers should make themselves familiar with these forms as it is essential to be able to spot any mistakes made after completing them. The majority of forms are now available in software programs. This enables staff to complete the forms looking at a computer screen and to amend any mistakes without difficulty. The completed form can then be elec-tronically transmitted directly to the parties requiring it and paper copies run off as required. In general, small importers obtaining goods from outside the EU will use clearing agents to clear goods through their place of entry into the UK as well as for deliveries to their premises.

SINGLE ADMINISTRATIVE DOCUMENT (SAD)

This is the document in general use between the UK and countries outside the European Union. It is usually not required for cross-bor-der trade for countries in the EU unless the goods originate from out-side the area. The SAD documents consist of a set of eight forms.

Copies of the SAD documents are printed by Customs and Excise departments and can be obtained from their local offices. The first three copies of the eight-form set are for use in export, numbers 4 and 5 for transit purposes and copies 6-8 for import usage.

Variations in the number of copies used do occur as not all will be used by exporters in every transaction. Some of the information may not be included with the documents travelling with the goods for commercial reasons and has to be provided separately by the importer. In practice, many importers prepare import declarations before the goods arrive in order to minimise delays. This is increasingly happening as importers input data electronically to the customs at those locations where they are computerised.

TARIC

The European Community has a common customs tariff (CCT) used for specifying rates of duty and a separate but related system for collecting statistics known as NIMEXE (the nomenclature for the external trade statistics of the EU). In addition, there is a nomenclature common coding system to satisfy all the needs of the EU. This is known as the harmonized commodity description and coding system (HS). There are up to 15 digits in the commodity code and each section of the code has a specific descriptive purpose. Customs and Excise publish a booklet describing the working of the code.

A full list of commodity codes, which occupy a number of large books, called the 'Tariff' is available at Customs and Excise offices and major Chambers of Commerce. It is not easy to understand these codes and businesses should seek help from freight forwarders and other experts in order to ensure the products they are importing have been assigned the correct code from about 15,000 different headings. It is essential that correct codes are assigned to products, otherwise incorrect import duties may be paid, resulting in overpayments or penalties for the incorrect coding and underpayment of duties.

One of the most complex areas of the classification of goods is the mechanical/electronics sector such as computer products.

Many products attract customs duty but there are a considerable number of duty exclusions which are eligible for duty suspensions and hence are free of duty. All Customs and Excise offices, freight forwarders, major Chambers of Commerce and some central libraries should have copies of this three-volume customs Tariff plus the updating customs notices. This integrated system described is known as Taric.

CERTIFICATES OF ORIGIN

The certificate of origin is a standard form completed by the supplier. It details the quantity and value of the goods being shipped and their place of manufacture. The supplier's Chamber of Commerce or another authorized authority authenticates the certificate and the signatory with its official stamp or seal. The person signing the certificate has to be registered with the authorizing body. The wording of the certificate has to match exactly that in the other documents. It includes the names and addresses of the exporter and importer, a description of the goods and their country of origin, and the signature and the seal or stamp of the authorizing body. Fortunately, many goods imported into the UK do not require a certificate of origin. A list of goods that do is available from Customs and Excise.

INSPECTION CERTIFICATES

It is becoming more common for importers to ask for preshipment inspection documents. The Société Générale de Surveillance SA (SGS) have set up a special organization to arrange for importers' goods to be inspected for quantity, quality and other matters to ensure they comply with the buyer's contract before they are shipped. Assuming the inspection is satisfactory, SGS will issue a clean report of findings (CRF) otherwise known as an SGS certificate. There are other organizations who also provide an inspection service in overseas countries.

ATA (ADMISSION TEMPORAIRE) CARNETS

An ATA carnet document permits the temporary import and re-export of certain goods for special purposes such as might be required for an exhibition. It avoids the need to pay duties and the need for full import and re-export documentation. ATA carnets cover such temporary imports from some 50 countries who are members of the ATA convention.

Suppliers within the EU should not need to use carnets, only those situated outside. They will usually obtain their carnets from their local Chamber of Commerce. Goods generally covered by carnets include those for exhibitions, trade samples and professional equipment.

SITPRO (SIMPLER TRADE PROCEDURES BOARD)

SITPRO works nationally and internationally to simplify trade documents and procedures. It is an independent organization closely linked to the government and strongly supported by the DTI. SITPRO provide an extensive range of services covering international trader documentation and systems. From time to time they organize free seminars and discussion days for international traders at various centres in the UK. Information publications, such as a letter of credit checklist, are available from SITPRO. They have also developed computerized document systems and standards for electronic data interchange (EDI) for use between traders and organizations such as banks and work closely with the Electronic Commerce Association.

SITPRO provide training for import and export staff in documentary procedures. Should a company be planning to develop their own unit for handling documentary systems, eg those relating to the import and clearance of goods, they should contact SITPRO for information and advice. SITPRO have a register of approved consultants who can help companies establish approved systems, particularly those using computers.

VAT

The Excise and Inland Customs Advice Centres provide information and advice on VAT matters as well as on customs and excise duties and procedures. These centres carry a good stock of VAT notices and leaflets from which importers can select those which are relevant to their business. It is essential to acquire a good grasp of how VAT applies to imports to ensure that it is only paid on goods to which it is applicable. For example, VAT applies to adult clothing but not to children's clothing.

VAT is charged on the importation of goods at the same rate as the same goods supplied in the UK. This applies whether or not the person importing the goods is registered for VAT. It is chargeable on the customs value of the goods plus any other duties or charges. The VAT is paid at the same time as other customs duties and charges are paid. All these can be paid outright at importation or under duty deferment arrangements for which one applies to the Central Department Office in Southend on Sea. All import VAT is treated as input tax and may be set against your output tax provided it is all within your business.

The value for VAT of imported goods is the same as their customs value. This is determined by the customs rule set out in their notice on the valuation of imported goods for customs purposes. If your imports are of sufficiently high value, the Customs Handling Import Export Freight (CHIEF) computer will calculate the value for VAT by adding any duties, levies, additional costs, etc to the value declared on the import declaration, ie the import copies of the SAD set. This import entry must be presented at the customs entry processing unit (EPU) or entry processing point (EPP) where the goods are to be cleared. If the value for VAT is below that which CHIEF would normally calculate, you must calculate manually the amount of VAT payable.

Currently, on cross-border trade within the EU, VAT is paid by the purchaser, whereas in due time, if everything proceeds as planned, it will be paid by the originator of the invoice. The purchaser must declare the VAT applicable to his imported goods, whether from the EU or outside, as part of his input tax. If the latter exceeds his output tax, he may still have to pay some balancing VAT, taking into account he will already have paid VAT on goods imported from outside the EU but not yet on those from the countries within. Importers of goods from EU suppliers who are VAT exempt (because their annual turnover is too small) do not pay VAT on acquisitions.

Should the supplier be registered for VAT his invoices must show his VAT number and the VAT number of his customer, ie the importer, as well as the normal details required on a VAT invoice. The purchaser charges VAT on his purchases as an acquisition, showing it in a separate box on his normal VAT return. He claims deductions for VAT on the same return. It is essential for an importer to ensure that all his potential suppliers from EU countries have details of his VAT number.

WAREHOUSING

Importers can have their supplies delivered to an approved warehouse to await their needs. While goods are in the warehouse, import duties and VAT do not have to be paid. These charges are usually payable when the goods are removed from the warehouse. These facilities are also available for excise goods and for CAP (Common Agricultural Policy) goods imported from other countries within the EU. Customs and Excise issue a variety of notices regarding warehousing and copies of those relevant to your business can be obtained from them.

Goods can also be held in a free zone without paying import charges or VAT. If excise duty is applicable, these goods must still be held in an approved excise warehouse. Duties and VAT must be paid when the goods are either consumed within the free zone or moved into the UK market. There is no VAT or duties applicable in the UK when the goods are moved from the free zone or approved warehouses to another EU country or to a country outside the EU. Goods imported to and exported from a warehouse will usually be processed using a single administrator document set. It is probable that most of the information required by Customs and Excise will be processed electronically direct to their CHIEF computer. Information on CHIEF is available on the Internet, as well as in publications obtainable from HM Customs and Excise office.

IMPORT LICENSING

One of the main tasks of the import office is to obtain import licences when they are required. This effectively applies to many products bought from countries outside the EU. Most goods in free circulation within the EU do not require a licence for their import into the UK. Many goods that do require a licence do not have to be imported with a specific import licence but they can be brought into the UK under an open general import licence (OGIL), which allows you to import them without applying for a separate licence for each consignment. If they are specified in the schedule to the OGIL then you do require a specific import licence.

Copies of the OGIL and the associated schedules, which make up a large volume of information, can be obtained from HM Stationery Office and major booksellers, or they may be available for study in a large trade reference library. The OGIL schedules will tell you if there are restrictions on the goods you wish to import.

Information on import licensing procedures and changes to the OGIL can be found in 'Notices to Importers' which are published from time to time in the Thursday edition of Lloyd's List or by contacting the DTI's Import Licensing Branch.

All goods imported into the UK and not in free circulation in the EU must be declared to Customs. Anyone requiring information about import licensing should contact the Import Licensing Branch of the DTI at Billingham. A free copy of 'A Guide to Import Licensing' is also available from this branch of the DTI.

TEXTILE AND CLOTHING LICENCES

The majority of import restrictions operated by the DTI apply to textiles and clothing, iron and steel, and firearms and ammunition. Textile and clothing importers are fairly widespread in the UK as might be expected from the decline in the textile industry. Most of the restrictions on imports of textiles and clothing from outside the European Union come under the Multi-Fibre Arrangement (MFA). The MFA consists of a series of bilateral agreements between the EU and a number of exporting countries, setting out quotas for their exports to the UK. The quota levels are managed by the European Commission in Brussels and the licensing authorities in member states using computer links to Brussels. Licences against textile quotas are valid for up to six months from the date of issue. The licence expires at the end of the quota period but it can be extended.

The MFA is gradually being phased out under the regulations of the World Trade Organization (WTO) agreement on textiles and clothing.

PREFERENCES

Preferences in duty terminology means that you pay a lower rate of import customs duty or none at all on the goods you import. A list of preference countries can be obtained from Customs and Excise. It is published in Volume 1 of the Customs and Excise Tariff. Countries such as the African, Caribbean and Pacific States (ACPS) and the Overseas Countries and Territories (OCTS) as well as the Maghreb countries (Algeria, Morocco and Tunisia) and the EEA and EFTA countries still not in the European Union, ie Iceland, Norway and Switzerland, appear in this list.

The list of goods which are eligible for preference and their rates of duty are published in Volume 2 of the Tariff. Changes to preferential arrangements sometimes take place at very short notice but customs clearing agents with access to the Customs and Excise clearing facility can advise you very quickly. Otherwise, it is necessary to watch the information that is posted on the noticeboards of the customs entry processing units (EPUs). The preferential rate for Common Agricultural Policy (CAP) charges can be obtained from the Intervention Board for Agricultural Products in Reading.

In some cases there are restrictions on the quantity of certain goods that can be imported under preference. These are known as ceilings or tariff quotas; details are published in Volume 1 of the Tariff and some notices. All preference goods must meet the origin rules, ie the products must be wholly produced in the preference country or manufactured from imported materials that required an acceptable level of processing. You may require information from your supplier to ensure that his goods satisfy these rules.

There are three main types of document covering the import of goods to which preference applies. These are Form EUR1, an invoice declaration, and Form A. The last is used for imports from the generalized system of preferences (GSP) countries (see p 85-6). All other preference countries use form EUR1. The invoice declaration is a simplified form of documentation that can be used in place of the EUR1. It consists of a declaration, usually on the back of the invoice, although it can be on some of the other documents such as the consignment note. This declaration made by the importer states that the goods meet the rules of origin. The exporter states that the goods conform to the preferential trade arrangement with the UK or the EU, and the country of origin of the goods.

An importer looking for sources of supply should check whether the goods he requires are available under the preference rules from one of the preference receiving countries and whether or not they are subject to duty from other sources.

QUOTAS

A number of countries conduct their trade to some extent using a bilateral trading system. Similarly, the EU has a number of product areas, eg textiles and bananas, in which it operates quota systems. In effect, this means there is an agreement between the parties either to limit the amount of a product that will be imported into the EU or there is an agreed volume of trade under a bilateral agreement between the two countries. Bilateral agreements normally specify the products and services included in the agreement. The trade is normally regulated by the issue of import and export licences. Importers should always check before placing orders where quotas apply that the quota has not already been fully utilized and that they can import what they require. The Import Licensing Branch in the UK normally issues import licences against export certificates. Details of licensing arrangements for quota goods and quota levels are published in 'Notices to Importers' which appear in the Lloyd's List, Thursday edition.

Quota licensing

Export Administered Quotas are those controlled by the exporting country which allocates the quota by the issue of export certificates. The UK importer must present the export certificate with his application for an import licence. Most licensing, including all licensing under the MFA (see p 50), comes within this category.

Import Administered Quotas mainly relate to non-textile imports from non-MFA agreement countries such as China and North Korea. The licensing arrangements are authorized by the European Commission in accordance with rules and regulations laid down by the Council and the Commission. The quotas and licensing arrangements are published in 'Notices to Importers' at the beginning of each quota period.

Surveillance licensing is used where there are no set quota limits but when there may be agreed restraint limits. Double-control surveillance licensing means that import licences will only be issued against importers' applications supported by a firm order and certificate of origin; no export certificate is required from the exporting country.

CUSTOMS PROCEDURES - CFSP

The fundamentals of customs procedures have not changed significantly in respect of goods coming to the UK from countries outside the EU. The main principles are as follows:

- Goods must be imported through places (ie ports, warehouses, depots) approved by customs.
- The carrier must lodge information with customs prior to unloading.
- All goods must be properly reported to customs, ie entered, and all duties, levies, VAT and other charges paid before the goods are released.

- Customs staff may examine all goods to check that they conform to the entry statement.

Currently, most import entries are input electronically, and as a result Customs and Excise have developed a system to facilitate the movement of non-EC imports and exports. The system, The Electronic Data Capture Service (EDCS), uses the electronic data interchange (EDI) system and enables authorized traders to control their international trading activities with the minimum of customs intervention. There are four main elements in the Customs Freight Simplified Procedures (CFSP):

- The trader must be authorized and satisfy a standard set of criteria.
- The Simplified Frontier Declaration (SFD) will need to be supplied to customs by EDI.
- A supplementary declaration imports (SDI) must be sent by EDI within ten days of the import of the goods.
- A systems audit will be carried out by customs to verify that all revenue and statistics are accounted for correctly.
- A trader will need to apply to his local Excise and Inland Customs Advice Centre to be authorized. There is no minimum trading turnover requirement so any trader can apply for authorization.

Simplified Frontier Declaration – SFD

Once goods have arrived and any smuggling and regulatory checks have been carried out, they will be released after customs have accepted the SFD. The SFD consists of the following information:

- Importer's unique trade reference (TURN)*
- Importer's commercial reference
- Declarant's TURN
- Declarant's commercial reference
- Commercial description of the goods
- Controlled goods identifier (CGI)
- Customs procedure identifier (CPI)
- Inventory system identification code (inventory ports only)
- Inventory systems reference (inventory ports only)
- Location of goods/port of arrival
- Arrival indicator (non-inventory ports only)
- Container number (non-inventory ports only)
- Vehicle registration number or marks and numbers (non-inventory ports only).

* The Trader Unique Reference Number (TURN).

The SFD can be transmitted to customs by the authorised CFSP importer or by a third party such as a freight forwarder, carrier or computer bureau.

The CSD (I) consists of the information that is required by customs in order to enable them to compile fiscal and statistical information. It also enables customs to calculate and secure the revenue due once the information has been validated. They will advise the revenue due per declaration.

A booklet describing the Customs freight simplified procedures can be obtained from Excise and Inland Customs Advice Centres.

7

Freight Documents

All importers should have a good understanding of the freight documents used in international trade. Failure to understand them can result in delivery delays. The most important documents are described below.

BILL OF LADING

The bill of lading relates to the contract of carriage, ie the contract for the transport of goods. The contract is normally between the shipper and the shipowner. It is evidence of a contract of carriage, a receipt of goods from the carrier and currently a document of title. The latter is likely to cease to apply with the advent of the electronic transmission of data. Currently, the title to the goods can be transferred by the endorsement and delivery of the bill of lading. There are a number of different forms and types of bills of lading:

A *received bill of lading* is one in which the word 'shipped' does not appear. In effect, it is a 'received for shipment bill' in that the goods have simply been handed over to the shipowner. Shipped (on board) bills of lading usually contain the preprinted words 'shipped in apparent good order and condition' and confirm the goods are on board the vessel.

A *through bill of lading* implies two or more carriers will be involved in getting the goods to their destination. A *transshipment bill of lading* is similar and means that there is no direct service between two ports en route and the shipowner has to transship the goods via an intermediate port. This occurs with containers which are transshipped via an intermediate port such as Singapore to other less well served destinations.

A *stale bill of lading* is one that is presented late. Bills presented to importers (consignees or their banks) after the goods have arrived are said to be stale. The effect of bills being late is to delay the clearance of goods from the port, warehouses or depot and additional ware-housing charges may be incurred.

A *groupage bill of lading* arises when a forwarding agent groups together various suppliers' consignments, which may be going to different consignees, for despatch in an LCL (less than full container load) container. The shipowner issues a groupage bill of lading while the forwarding agent will issue to individual consignors a certificate of shipment sometimes called the 'house' bill of lading.

A *clean bill of lading* has no notations on it and means the goods have been received and/or shipped in good condition and in the right quantity. A bill which is issued by the shipowner and which is 'clean' or 'underclaused' means the shipowner accepts full liability for the cargo.

A *claused bill of lading* is one to which the shipowner has added a statement to the effect the goods are not as described, eg are incorrectly packed, or damaged or broken in some way. This type of claused bill of lading will often not be acceptable to a bank.

A *negotiable bill of lading* contains the words 'or his or their assigns' or some variation thereon. This allows the goods to be transferred by endorsement and delivery to other parties to the transaction; each party to the transaction would have to endorse the back of the bill to take delivery of the goods.

Importers should be aware of the different types of bill of lading they are likely to receive.

The following are typical of the details likely to appear on a bill of lading:

1. Name of the shipper, usually the exporter or his agent.
2. Name of the ship.
3. Complete description of the goods including package number, contents, dimensions, gross weight and package markings.
4. Marks and numbers with the goods to which they relate.
5. Shipping port.
6. Discharge port.
7. Details of freight charges and when and where they are to be paid.
8. Consignee's name.
9. Contract of carriage terms.
10. Date goods received for shipment and date loaded on the ship.
11. Name and address of the person to be notified about the arrival of the ship at the port of destination. This is usually the importer and/or his agent.
12. Number of bills of lading relating to the consignment signed by the ship's master or his agent as the receipt for the goods.
13. Signature of the ship's master or his agent.

A *short form of bill of lading* is one that does not show the shipping company's terms and conditions of carriage on its reverse side. Normally, three copies of the bills of lading are issued: one for the exporter, another for the shipping company and the third for you, the importer.

AIR WAYBILL

An air waybill is an air freight arrangement document. It is not a document of title and cannot be transferred or negotiated. Essentially, it is a receipt for goods despatched and evidence of the conditions of carriage. There are usually 12 copies of the air waybill of which the first three copies are known as the originals. The conditions of carriage are shown on the back of the air waybill. A standard International Air Transport Association (IATA) air waybill is used throughout the world. This contains the following details:

1. Date and place of execution.
2. Departure and destination airports by name.
3. Consignor, consignee and first carrier's name, addresses and account numbers.
4. Description of the goods.
5. Number of packages with the dimensions, weight and markings for each one.
6. Freight charge details.
7. Declared values of goods and carriage for customs purposes.
8. Date of flight and other flight details including those for any additional carrier.
9. Signature of the shipper, eg the exporter or his agent.
10. Signature of the carrier (airline) or his agent.

The exporter or whoever is responsible for booking the shipment must give correct and complete instructions to the airline or their agent. A standard shipper's letter of instruction is used for this purpose. Gradually, all this documentation is being handled electronically using computers and standard EDI formats. Information on these formats can be obtained from SITPRO, appropriate computer software suppliers and the airlines.

CMR NOTE

The CMR note is an international consignment document which is required for all movements of goods by road which involve transit across frontiers. It is usually completed by the supplier. Three copies are required, one for the supplier, ie the exporter, one for retention by the carrier and one which accompanies the goods, until they reach their destination, eg the importer's premises.

CIM NOTE

The CIM note is an international consignment note for the move-ment of goods by rail under one document. It is completed by the supplier, his agent or the first rail carrier. There are six copies of the document: the original, the invoice and the arrival copy are the most important. The advantage of this standard document is that it is sub-ject to a common code of conditions for different rail networks so there is no intermediate handling of the freight and no customs examination in transit countries.

SSN (STANDARD SHIPPING NOTE)

The standard shipping note is a six-part documentary set covering the delivery of goods to a UK port. When the exporter wishes to send his goods by ship he contacts the shipping company or its agent who will then send him a booking form and an SSN. The completion of the SSN tells the shipping company what happens to the goods when they reach the destination port, ie who will collect them, who will pay unloading charges and whether or not they are to go into a ware-house within the docks. The port authorities sign a copy of the SSN and this is returned to the exporter as proof of delivery. In effect, the SSN requires the port authority to receive and handle the shipment.

PARCEL POST

Companies who wish to send packages which are within the size and weight limits for international parcels should consider sending them by an international parcels service. In the UK, SITPRO provide docu-ment sets known as post packs for sending goods by parcel post. Your supplier will probably use similar post packs for sending parcels to you from his own country. Usually, any customs charges due are cal-culated on the basis of the customs declaration made by the sender and are collected by the postman when the package is delivered.

8

The Import Office

In a small business it is essential to have someone who is skilled and trained in handling all the administrative aspects of importing such as transport documents, purchasing and stock control. Efficient systems and a well-organized office are one of the keys to success.

The import purchasing units must liaise closely with the sales function if the imported goods are for resale, and with the production function if they are for incorporation in the company's own products or to be subjected to further processing. Clearly, purchases must be made in the right quantity at the right times and at an acceptable delivered cost if they are to meet the needs of both the production and sales units.

The purchasing unit must work closely with people in the sales and production units to ensure that they supply the correct technical specifications for the products to be imported. They will need to advise them of any product improvements, price changes or any other changes or opportunities that could benefit the business. The purchasing unit will need to liaise closely with the finance or accounting unit to ensure that money will be available when required to pay for imports. The accountants will need to know the delivered cost and how long goods are likely to be in stock in order to calculate correctly the costs of the imported goods into the manufacturing process or for resale.

OFFICE ORGANIZATION

The size of the import unit will grow as the business grows. Initially, it is likely to consist of an import manager responsible for arranging purchases and a documentation clerk. As the business expands an accounts clerk may also be required. At the beginning, purchases are likely to be made on a delivered, or CIF UK port or inland depot basis, but as the business develops it may become cheaper to buy on an ex-works basis, particularly from suppliers in the EU. This will entail more negotiation work with transport organizations, customs and insurance, and more documentation and hence, in due course, more staff.

DOCUMENTATION

The import office uses a variety of different forms, depending on the extent to which it engages in the transport arrangements, and these depend on its buying terms.

If it buys ex-works, it will be responsible for the movement of the goods from the supplier's premises and will require a variety of forms from a trade stationery supplier or from the freight forwarder. In all purchasing contracts it should be clear who initiates and who completes the forms. Normally, the supplier will initiate the following:

● Invoices
● Certificates of origin
● Bills of exchange
● Dangerous goods shipping notes (seven-part set)
● Standard shipping notes (ten-part set).

Your freight forwarder, carrier or you, if you are directly arranging transport, will need a stock of blank forms such as:

● FIATA bills of lading
● House air waybills
● Neutral air waybills
● Sea waybills
● CMR consignment notes (for goods sent by road)
● CIM consignment notes (for goods sent by rail)
● Import licence forms.

FIATA is the International Federation of Forwarding Agents and FIATA bills of lading are internationally recognized bills. SITPRO have comprehensive information available relating to the movement of goods. While their approved computer software system providers concentrate on the export process, some of them have or are developing systems for importers. SITPRO publish a number of booklets and leaflets and a regular newsletter, 'Sitpronews'. These are available from SITPRO or their distributors.

The import licence forms are freely available from the Import Licensing Branch of the DTI along with their booklet, 'A Guide to Import Licensing'. Other forms and stationery can be obtained from business stationery shops although traders usually obtain their requirements from specialist stationery suppliers.

The office should also ensure they receive publications and other regular international newsletters from their banks, for example the National Westminster Bank publish a monthly International Trade Bulletin. Customs and Excise publish a newsletter which will help to ensure that the office keeps up to date on customs developments. The International Chamber of Commerce (ICC) have publications of which the office should have copies such as those concerning

Incoterms, uniform customs and practice for documentary credits and uniform rules for collections.

TRAINING

The importance of training staff in an import operation should not be underestimated. Those involved in the actual purchasing should have a thorough knowledge of their products. They should have had training in purchasing and be fluent in at least one overseas language relevant to the markets from which they purchase. Knowledge of all the terms used in international trade relating to payment, banking, insurance, transport and customs is essential. Even if the exporter is responsible for most of the contract arrangements, it is essential for the purchaser to ensure they satisfy his requirements. Several organizations provide suitable training.

Chambers of Commerce

Chambers of Commerce are the biggest providers of short-term training in many aspects of international trade through their seminars, workshops and other events. They are the leading providers of seminars on international trade documentation and import offices should make sure they are aware of their activities. The larger Chambers provide much more extensive programmes than smaller ones. They also run activities relating to specific countries, often in conjunction with the DTI and other bodies. The DTI also run a series of events on individual countries for some of which there is no charge. Details of these meetings, seminars and workshops can be obtained from local DTI regional offices.

STANDARDS AND SPECIFICATIONS

The import office should keep records of all standards and specifications for the products it is responsible for purchasing. Although a considerable amount of work has been done to harmonize technical standards within the EU, work still remains to be done. It is therefore still important within the EU to check that any products to be purchased will be manufactured to conform with UK standards and other regulatory requirements in respect of such matters as health and safety. It is even more important, when buying from countries outside the EU, to ensure the product you propose purchasing will not contravene any UK requirement, otherwise you may not be able to use or resell it.

The British Standards Institution (BSI), trade associations and the appropriate government department are the organizations with whom contact should be maintained to keep up to date with changes in standards and regulations. BSI have a very large information base from which they can tell you if the product you wish to buy is likely to conform with UK standards. Naturally, you will need to give them the fullest information about your source of supply and the product you propose to buy.

The information in this chapter should help any importer to check that his import unit is trained to carry out the work required, including maintaining contact with other organizations and keeping themselves up to date.

9

The European Union

The development and expansion of the European Union has important implications for importers. The progress towards the harmonization of standards and safety requirements, the removal of trade barriers and the simplification of trade procedures provides increasing opportunities to find new sources of supply. The expansion of the EU and the integration of new countries into the Union also opens up new purchasing possibilities.

The EU now consists of 15 countries, the last to join being Austria, Finland and Sweden. The other 12 are: the UK, Ireland, Germany, France, Luxembourg, the Netherlands, Belgium, Italy, Spain, Portugal, Denmark and Greece. Switzerland has decided not to join but will still have European Free Trade Area (EFTA) status, while Norway and Iceland, the other non-joiners, have European Economic Area (EEA) status. There is a slight difference between the way goods from Switzerland are treated compared with goods from Norway and Iceland. None of these countries has the same status as an EU country and it is important to check the procedure requirements with Customs and Excise before arranging imports from any of them.

SINGLE MARKET INFORMATION

It is important to know what EU Directives are proposed and which Directives are being enforced in the UK and in your supplier's country within the EU that may affect your business. This information is often available from your trade association, Chamber of Commerce or the DTI. In addition, it can be obtained from the EU's CELEX database which can be accessed through the Financial Times Profile system or through the DTI database known as Spearhead.

EU Directives eventually become regulations in the UK and all other EU countries but not necessarily at the same time. One of the most important concerns consumer protection in regard to general product safety. Make sure you and your EU suppliers are familiar with these regulations which in the UK are covered by the Statutory Instrument 1994 No 2328. This is described in 'The General Product Safety Regulations 1994', a copy of which can be obtained from HM Stationery Office.

HARMONIZATION

The harmonization of quality standards, safety requirements, fiscal and other regulations is a continual process within the single market. At any time there are a number of EU legislative measures being adopted, in discussion or proposed, as well as those already adopted which may be of importance to your company. Different quality standards in other countries are still a hindrance to free trade and the EU is gradually harmonizing them. However, some countries are still likely to adopt new requirements independently, particularly in the health and environmental fields, which are obstacles to free trade. The European Commission has had some success in opposing such regulations.

Over 100 technical committees are responsible to the EU. Its commissions are responsible for establishing common standards and methods of testing to meet the requirements of various EU Directives which establish essential requirements for health, safety and consumer protection. The British Standards Institution (BSI) acts for the UK on these committees. It has and needs UK company representatives on them who are nominated through their trade associations. It will thus be apparent that the BSI can advise on the status of any existing or proposed harmonization of standards and rules in the technical areas.

Intellectual property rights, ie patents, trade marks and copyright, are protected in most EU countries. Whereas gradually it will be possible to register these rights at central community offices, in many cases it is still necessary to register them in each individual country. An importer should be aware whether or not his EU supplier has registered his rights in the UK and that the registration is displayed on goods and individual product packages when necessary.

The EU has a common commercial policy covering trade relations with outside countries. There are common external tariffs which apply to imports into the Community of non-EU goods. The Community is obliged to set or modify its rules in accordance with the requirements of the General Agreement on Tariffs and Trade (GATT) and the Organization for Economic Cooperation and Development (OECD). Information on these matters can be obtained from the DTI's External European Policy Division. Changes in the EU tariffs and regulations can be obtained from *Croner's Reference Book for Importers* and their regular 'Importer's Briefing Newsletter', which is of great value to many importers as it keeps them up to date with any changes that might affect their business.

Importers should be aware that the General System of Preferences (GSP), which implies a lower or nil rate of import customs duty if certain criteria are satisfied, applies to countries which have special associations with the EU. Information on any particular country's preferences with the EU can be obtained from the appropriate DTI Country Desk or from Excise and Inland Customs Advice Centres.

SMALL COMPANIES

The Community has a number of programmes to assist small companies throughout the Union. The European Information Centres (EICs) are required to provide small and medium-sized enterprises with information on EU market intelligence, research and development programmes, finance and training. The Small Business Task Force in Brussels provides EICs with basic and up-to-date Community documentation and access to certain EU databases. The centres help small and medium-sized enterprises (SMEs) to find contacts in EU countries, with applications to participate in EU programmes and assist with the formalities. They also provide information on new EC legislation and updates on the harmonization of product standards. They hold copies of all official EC documents. Many of the EICs are associated with Chambers of Commerce who, like the DTI regional offices, can tell you how to contact them.

BC-NET

The purpose of Business Cooperation Network (BC-Net) is to assist small and medium-sized enterprises in different countries within the European Community to find contacts for collaboration. Run by the Business Cooperation Centre (BCC) in Brussels, it is essentially a computerized system which links a few hundred business advisers throughout the Union. These advisers are the first point of contact in the UK for any SME interested in finding a partner for any type of legitimate business activity. This includes cooperative agreements, joint ventures, licences, franchises, subcontracting agents, import and export arrangements and mergers.

For a fee, the adviser will offer some business planning advice and endeavour to find a suitable partner through the computerized network. A company or cooperation profile for an offer or request is drawn up by the adviser and fed into the BCC computer. If a match is found, the requesting UK company and the offering company are advised. If there is no match on the computer then all the advisers in the specified country or region are notified of the request. The advantage of BC-Net is that it brings companies together to participate in:

- Community research and development programmes;
- regional development and redevelopment activities;

- transnational subcontracting;
- joint ventures.

Finance for some of these activities may be available from the European Venture Capital Association (EVCA) and the European Investment Bank (EIB). The DTI's Small Firms Unit and Business Links Division should also be able to advise on any financial assistance that may be available.

PAYMENT TERMS

Most of the business in Europe is done on an open account basis. However, where the two parties to the transaction are not confident in each other, some measure of cash payment in advance of the despatch of goods may be required. In other instances, avalized bills of exchange may be requested in conjunction with documentary collection procedures. The latter are not easy to operate as many goods are now delivered direct to purchasers by road. Purchasers should always check carefully the trustworthiness and creditability of their potential suppliers, especially when they are asked for payment before they have received and been able to inspect the goods physically. Purchasers should always check on potential suppliers through their banks, credit rating agencies and possibly by talking to companies who already buy from them. If at all possible, visit your supplier in his office, warehouse and/or factory before buying.

EUROPEAN SINGLE MARKET

In January 1995 the single market consisted of 15 countries with a total population of about 350 million. Each country has its own characteristics and culture as well as regional variations. It is necessary to know each country in which you wish to make purchases as well as individual suppliers if a long and lasting business is to be built. The DTI regional offices and the DTI's EMIC library have booklets available such as 'Country Profiles and Hints to Exporters' which importers will find useful. Specific information can also be obtained from the DTI Country Desks and the EMIC library.

The following pages give a brief snapshot of each of the countries in the European single market. Much more market research should be undertaken if you are planning to trade with any of them.

GERMANY

The Federal Republic of Germany (FRG) is one of the world's leading economies. It has a population of about 80 million and has the strongest economy in Europe. The population enjoys a high standard of living and has a considerable reputation for hard work. Germany has excellent road, rail and air networks with good communication to other countries in Europe, and reliable air and sea communications to more distant lands.

The national language is German, with English as the second language for many people, except for those near the Danish border where Danish is second and those near the French border where it is French. While many Germans will no doubt use their English in negotiating with UK importers, the latter will find it in their interest to have a German-English interpreter unless they are fluent German speakers or are confident that the German sellers are fluent in English. German business people like correspondence to be in German so that they know exactly the terms to which they are agreeing in any contract. However, the seller will undoubtedly accept correspondence in English in order to achieve sales.

The German economy is the third most productive in the world after the USA and Japan. For this reason it is not surprising that the Deutsche Mark (DM) has been one of the strongest in the world. This will affect importers who are buying in Deutsche Marks, since it has steadily strengthened over the years against the pound sterling (although more recently it has fallen). German importers prefer to be paid in DM but will accept sterling payments.

Importers should be aware that German exporters will expect them to make a good impression, for example by being dressed smartly for business meetings. Appointments should be made well in advance and should not be changed. Punctuality is also important. Titles such as Herr Doktor or Frau Doktor are quite normal between business contacts. Shaking hands is customary and normal courtesies should be observed. If invited to your seller's home, it is normal to give the hostess a bunch of flowers which should be uneven in number and should not include red roses.

German exports to the UK mainly consist of machinery and vehicles. However, there are many other products available which the UK imports such as textiles. This is not surprising since Germany is the largest producer of finished textiles in Europe. The former West Germany is a major area of industrial production with large car and chemical manufacturing plants and a rapidly growing advanced technology industry in mechanical, electrical and electronic products. The service sector in computing, biotechnology, information processing and media is also very substantial. The major problem facing potential UK buyers is likely to be the price of goods because of the strength of the DM. However, advanced machine tools could be an attractive buy on an overall value basis.

The Kompass directory for Germany is just one of many which can help UK buyers looking for suppliers of specific products. Many important trade fairs, some of them international, take place in Germany and information about them can be obtained from your trade association, the Export Services Directorate of the DTI, your Chamber of Commerce and major business libraries.

FRANCE

The largest country in Europe in terms of area, its population at just under 60 million is substantially below that of Germany, about the same as that of Italy and slightly below that of the UK. In spite of its current economic problems, eg high levels of unemployment, it is the fourth strongest economy in the world. It is the leading agricultural producer in Europe. It is well known for its production of wine, cheese, fruit and various processed foods. It has a strong industrial sector particularly in steel, motor vehicles, aircraft, mechanical and electrical engineering, textiles, chemicals and food processing. In addition, it has a very large nuclear power industry and is a world leader in computing and telecommunications. Tourism is very important in France and UK tourist companies will be well aware of the opportunities for promoting holidays in France especially now the Channel Tunnel is operating.

Business people in France expect to conduct their business in French although often good at speaking English. Naturally, they will make the best use of their English if they are trying to sell to UK customers. French business people do not seem to mind if correspondence is in English since they place less emphasis on the written word than their German counterparts. Calling cards and prior appointments are expected and shaking hands and, more familiarly, the kissing of both cheeks are the usual forms of greeting. Meal times are often long and leisurely.

Paris is the world's leading conference city and UK importers wishing to make contacts in certain industrial and commercial sectors find such conferences a very fruitful source. Some major international exhibitions are held annually in Paris and as all the world knows, it is still the leading centre for fashion and associated accessories, eg perfumes. France is an important producer of textiles and several of its textile companies have associated and subsidiary companies in the former French colonies overseas such as the Ivory Coast and Morocco.

The Kompass country directory is a very useful reference for UK importers looking for French suppliers but there are many other good sources of information and help such as that available from the French Chambers of Commerce in Great Britain and the Chambers of Commerce in France.

The currency in France is the French Franc (FFr) but it has been more or less tied to the D Mark for a long time. It tends to be overvalued because of French government attempts to keep it tied to the DM through the Exchange Rate Mechanism (ERM). Importers need to decide, should they have the choice, whether they wish to pay in

French Francs or sterling, and expert advice should be sought from the international division of any of the major clearing banks.

ITALY

The population of Italy is similar in number to that of the UK and France, about 60 million, but occupies a land area about 25 per cent greater than that of the UK. Northern Italy, which is the most industrialized area of the country, is also the most prosperous. It has very few raw materials and has to rely on its exports to pay for them. Although it has a good agricultural industry it is heavily supported by the European Union's Common Agricultural Policy (CAP). The south of Italy is still very dependent on the agricultural industry and is poorer than the centre and the north.

Imports of Italian wine and processed foods are well known in the UK, but in fact Italy is heavily dependent on its exports of manufactured goods to pay for its material imports. Its export of vehicles is well known, but it also exports many manufactured goods such as industrial machinery, aircraft, chemicals, electronics, textiles, shoes and clothing. It also has an important jewellery manufacturing industry. The tourist industry is a major foreign currency earner both in the winter and in the warmer months. Italy trades strongly with other Mediterranean countries as well as with other members of the EU.

Importers visiting Italy should be aware that Milan, Turin and Genoa form the industrial triangle of Italy and that the important business centres are Bologna, Florence, Padua, Rome, Verona and Vicenza. Reference should be made to trade directories when planning a visit and appointments made beforehand. In London the Italian Trade Centre and the Italian Chamber of Commerce for Great Britain are good sources of help and information. Many fairs and exhibitions are held in the major business centres, details of which can be obtained from either of these two sources or from the *Directory of International Trade Fairs and Exhibitions* (published by MNA Verlag GmbH).

The currency of Italy is the Italian Lira (LIT). The country has suffered from bad periods of inflation and political instability and seems always to be fighting crime and corruption often associated with the mafia. In order to do business a knowledge of Italian is a distinct advantage; however many Italian business people do speak English especially those trying to do business with the UK. Prior appointments are essential if you are planning to visit Italy to meet potential suppliers.

SPAIN

The Spanish economy is the eighth largest in the world, according to its Gross National Product (GNP). It is a major industrial European economy with a large agricultural sector. It has a population of about 40 million which occupies a land area much larger than that of the UK. Since it joined the EU in 1986 some of its old-established industries such as shipbuilding, steel and textiles have declined. However, it has been very successful in expanding its chemical, electronics, information technology and industrial design sectors. It also manufactures vehicles and vehicle parts, some of which are already imported into the UK.

The Spanish agricultural sector is particularly known for its production of cereals, vegetables, citrus fruit, olive oil and wine. The warmer climate on the southern coast of Spain has enabled it to develop an all-year-round market garden type of industry. It is particularly able to supply other countries of the EU with spring vegetables, flowers and soft fruit before their own crops are ready. The Spanish processed food industry has also expanded rapidly. Tourism is a major contributor to the economy and the UK tourist trade has taken full advantage of the opportunity to sell Spanish holidays.

The political system is stable but the high level of unemployment has caused problems. The Spanish currency, the Peseta (Pta), has weakened against the DM and is likely to continue to weaken until Spain solves its high unemployment problem. The import and export of local currency is still subject to declaration above certain levels.

Importers visiting Spain on business should be prepared to exchange visiting cards. They should also be smartly dressed and speak some Spanish even though most Spanish businesspeople speak English. Handshaking is the usual form of greeting and hospitality, chivalry and courtesy are important. Some important exhibitions and conferences are held in Spain. The Spanish Convention Bureau in Spain, which represents 14 major towns, as well as the Spanish Chamber of Commerce and the Spanish Embassy Commercial Office in London and the Canning House Library at 2 Belgrave Square can provide information on conferences and exhibitions as well as names and addresses of potential suppliers of goods that are of interest to a UK importer.

THE NETHERLANDS

The Netherlands has a population of about 15 million and is one of the most densely populated countries in the world. Most of its inhabitants and certainly the vast majority of its business community speak English and German. It is a very easy country with which to trade and has had a long trading association with the UK. It is the world's second largest agricultural exporter based upon its very intensive agricultural and horticultural industries. Dairy products, meat, vegetables and flowers are the main products.

Industry is well developed with all kinds of heavy engineering, production of petrochemicals and plastics, pharmaceuticals, synthetic fibres and steel. It also has a wide range of light industries including the manufacture of electronic goods and textiles. Industry is concentrated in the area bounded by Amsterdam, Rotterdam and The Hague. It has the largest port in Europe with very extensive warehouses for the storage and transshipment of goods coming from other countries. There is a very large container port with communications by inland waterways, eg the Rhine, motorways, and rail to other parts of Europe. Among its newer activities are the technological industries of computing, telecommunications and biotechnology.

Appointments are always necessary in the Netherlands and visiting cards should be exchanged at the first meeting. A high standard of dress is expected. Secretarial agencies are very common and a visiting UK importer should have no difficulty in finding the help he needs. Prior to the visit, information can be obtained from directories and from the Netherlands-British Chamber of Commerce. The Netherlands Convention Bureau in Holland and the usual sources in the UK can provide information on conferences and exhibitions. UK importers will also find traders in Holland who are suppliers of goods obtained from other parts of the world. Information on such companies should be available from local Chambers of Commerce in the main centres in the Netherlands.

BELGIUM AND LUXEMBOURG

Belgium and Luxembourg may be taken together as they have had an economic union for many years. Luxembourg is French speaking whereas Belgium is French, Dutch and German speaking. The language that is spoken varies from region to region. French is spoken by most businesspeople and English is either their second or third language. The two countries combined have a population of about 10 million. They are both densely populated and highly industrialized, although Luxembourg is now a major financial services centre. Both countries have a major steel industry which is in decline. Other traditional industries in Belgium, such as textiles, have also been in decline but new light industries have been developed. Manufactured goods and machinery are the largest exports. Brussels and Luxembourg are also important administrative centres for the EU.

The Belgian Franc (BFr) and the Luxembourg Franc (LFr) are on a par. UK importers will find Belgium and Luxembourg easy countries in which to do business. Service companies will find opportunities in Brussels and Luxembourg to act as UK representatives. Transport between the UK and Belgium is excellent; for travellers the Channel Tunnel has improved the direct communication between London and Brussels so one-day business visits are quite feasible. The transport of goods is easy by road, rail and using ro/ro ferries, container services or Le Shuttle via the Channel Tunnel. Antwerp is still one of the largest ports in the world with many traders and bonded warehouses.

Information on potential suppliers in the two countries can be obtained from the Belgian-Luxembourg Chamber of Commerce, the Belgian Embassy Commercial Section in London, the Brussels Chamber of Commerce, trade directories and trade magazines.

IRELAND

Agriculture is still the basis of the Irish economy although the industrial sector has grown rapidly in recent years. The population is about 3.5 million. Dublin, the capital city, is the main port and the commercial, industrial and trade centre. There are no language problems but there are cultural differences and UK importers should take care to get to know their potential suppliers.

Business is usually done on open account, as in the UK. Credit references and other company information can be readily obtained. Travel and transport between Ireland and the UK represent no problems. There are frequent ro/ro ferries as well as container shipments and airline services.   The Irish Punt (IR£) is still within the ERM but is worth less than the pound sterling. The main industrial sectors likely to be of interest to UK importers are food processing, textiles, chemicals and electronics. Information on possible suppliers can be obtained from the Irish Export Board in London and many other directory and trade magazine sources.

PORTUGAL

The population of Portugal is only 10 million. Nevertheless, it has shown great resilience since the loss of its overseas territories. Traditionally, the Portuguese economy has been based on agriculture, but it now has a large textile manufacturing sector and a significant footwear industry. Other significant products are wine, paper, cork and other wood products, electrical appliances, chemicals and ceramics. It also has a growing horticultural industry which supplies other European markets. The tourist industry continues to grow rapidly and tourist agents are able to offer UK customers good value Portuguese holidays.

The Portuguese currency is the Escudo (Esc) which has suffered in recent years from inflation. Nevertheless, because of low labour costs Portuguese products are attractive to many UK importers. Historically, Britain has been Portugal's main trading partner. Sources of help and information are the Portuguese Chamber of Commerce and Industry, the Portuguese Trade and Tourist Office in the UK, the Associaçao Commercial de Lisboa, in Portugal, and many publications.

DENMARK

Many English people regard Denmark as primarily an agricultural producer and certainly its pork products are well known in the UK.

However, Denmark's industry contributes more than three times as much as its agriculture to the GNP. Manufacturing companies tend to be small and highly specialized. Many are found in the food processing, drinks, metal, electronics, toys, ceramics and furniture industries. The country has a high standard of living but many of its companies are very efficient and their products are therefore attractive to UK importers.

The currency is the Danish Krone (DKr) and is reasonably strong. Many Danish businesspeople speak English and German and it is relatively easy to do business with them. Denmark has good air, road and sea communications and regular ro/ro ferries operate between Denmark and the UK. Information on Danish exporters and the goods they have to offer can be obtained from the Danish Embassy, Commercial Section and the Danish Trade Office in London.

GREECE

Greece has a population of only 10 million people and it is one of the poorest countries in the EU. The agricultural industry is still the main contributor to the country's GNP and it receives a lot of financial help from the EU. Greece has developed some important industrial sectors in textiles, clothing and shoes, cement, mining and metals, chemicals, steel and processed agricultural products. Large quantities of wheat, barley, maize, tobacco and fruit, including dried fruit, are exported. Tourism is the most important service industry and most UK travel agents offer Greek holidays either on the mainland or on some of the islands.

The Greek currency is the Drachma (Dr); however, it is one of the weakest currencies in the EU and UK buyers may be asked to pay by letter of credit in sterling. Athens, the capital, is the main commercial centre and over half the industry in Greece is concentrated in that area. Other industrial centres are found in Salonika, Patras, Volos and Larissa. Information on Greek exports can be obtained from the Economic and Commercial Sections of the Greek Embassy and the Athens Chamber of Commerce.

AUSTRIA

Austria finally joined the EU on 1 January 1995. It has always had very close links with Germany and the currency, the Austrian Schilling (ASch), is very closely tied to the D Mark. In contrast with its neighbours to the east, who were part of the Communist bloc, it has a very high standard of living. In fact, Austria is one of the most prosperous countries in the world. It has a highly successful agricultural and forestry industry and many companies process the crops. It has strong iron and steel, chemicals, metal working and engineering sectors. The tourist industry is very successful and many UK tourist agencies sell Austrian skiing holidays as well as specialist summer holidays.

Communications by road, rail and air to Austria are all good. Vienna is the capital, where about a fifth of the population of 8 million reside. Vienna is a major commercial and trading centre, especially for eastern Europe. In their business dealings, Austrian businesspeople are quite formal and, while many speak English, a working knowledge of German is an advantage. Information and advice on Austrian exporters can be obtained from the Austrian Trade Commission in London.

SWEDEN AND FINLAND

The other two countries to join the EU on 1 January 1995 were Sweden and Finland. The former has a population of nearly 9 million and the the latter one of 5 million. Both countries have extensive areas of forestry which play a major part in their economies. Timber, paper and wood products such as furniture feature in both countries' exports. Finland has a large engineering sector and is a major exporter of consumer goods. Sweden is a highly industrialized country which has suffered in recent years from the high costs of its social welfare. Besides its wood products, Sweden is a major exporter of vehicles, office and telecommunications equipment and chemicals.

The Swedish currency, the Swedish Krona (KSr), and the Finnish currency, Markka (FMk), have both suffered from being too tightly pegged to the European Exchange Rate Mechanism and have had to be devalued. Sweden has particularly suffered from its excessive budget deficits due to its internal economic policies.

Information on Swedish exporters can be obtained from the Swedish Trade Council and the Swedish Chamber of Commerce in London as well as from the Federation of Swedish Commerce and Trade in Stockholm. The Finland Trade Centre in London and the Central Chamber of Commerce of Finland, the Suomen Keskuskauppakamari are useful sources of information on Finnish exports and exporters.

SWITZERLAND, NORWAY AND ICELAND

The three former EFTA countries who have decided to remain outside the European Union are Switzerland, Norway and Iceland. There are some differences in documentary requirements for goods coming from those countries in comparison with other members of the EU. The Excise and Customs Inland Advice Centres should be able to tell you about the documentary requirements, as should those freight forwarders and clearers who are familiar with arrangements for freight movements between these countries and the UK.

Switzerland has long been known for its financial services and precision manufacturing, eg watches, and also for food processing and chemical manufacture. It specializes in producing precision and high technology products such as machine tools, printing and photographic equipment, electronic control and medical equipment. The Swiss Franc (SFr) has long been regarded as a strong and stable currency. Information on Swiss exports can be obtained from the Swiss Embassy and the Swiss National Association of Trade and Industry in Zurich.

Norway is well known for its fishing, oil and gas industries. It also produces wood products and has a strong energy sector; in recent years it has developed some high technology industries. The Norwegian currency, the Krone (NKr), is a strong currency which relates to the strength of the Norwegian economy. Fish products, wood products, and oil and gas are significant export earners. Most business can be done at the major population centres such as Oslo, which contains 10 per cent of the population, and Bergen.

Information on Norwegian exporters can be obtained from the Norwegian-British Chamber of Commerce, the Commercial Section of the Norwegian Embassy and the Norwegian Trade Council, all in London.

The third country, *Iceland*, has a small population of less than 300,000. The economy is still very dependent on the fishing industry. There is some income from the sale of minerals, and in recent years light industries have been developed producing blankets, knitwear, textiles and paints. The currency is the Iceland Krona (IKr) which has remained stable against the pound sterling. The UK is one of Iceland's main export markets. Information on its exporters and the products they offer can be obtained from the Icelandic Embassy in London and the Chamber of Commerce in Reykjavik.

The countries in the EU and those regularly associated with it are probably the easiest from which to find suppliers of many products. However, products of better quality may be available from other developed countries in the rest of the world and lower in price from some of the developing countries where labour costs are low.

10

Industrialized Countries

This chapter looks at importing opportunities with the industrialized countries outside the European Union, the most important of which are Japan and USA, the world's two leading economies. To import from any of these countries, an open general import licence (OGIL) or specific import licence may be required. To find which you need, determine the coding for the products you wish to import from the harmonized commodity description and coding system (HS) product code books and contact the Import Licensing Branch of the DTI who will then tell you which type of licence you need and send you appropriate application forms. The OGIL allows you to import without having to apply for a licence every time you wish to import your product requirements.

The single administrative document (SAD) is now used by all the developed countries but you should check with your suppliers that they will use the SAD sets. In general, developed countries have strong currencies and will accept payment in their currency or sterling. Terms of payment will vary according to your ability to satisfy the exporter as to your creditworthiness and payment reliability. If you are buying from reputable companies, you should have no difficulties with quality, specifications or delivery terms. The developed countries are at the forefront of research and development in many industries and importers should be alert to improvements and new products.

A global view is necessary if you wish to be a leading importer in the eyes of your customers. Even in dealings with companies in developed countries you should always be alert to the possibility of fraud. Large companies, especially large multinational companies, tend to be more reliable suppliers than small companies, although if the latter are specialist exporters you may get a particularly good service.

UNITED STATES OF AMERICA

The USA is the world's most powerful economy. It has a population of over 255 million and, with major ports on both the Atlantic and

Pacific oceans, it is well positioned to take advantage of the European markets as well as the growing markets in the Pacific Far East. In partnership with Canada and Mexico, the USA comprises the North American Free Trade Agreement (NAFTA). The greatest concentration of industrial and commercial activity is in three major areas: New York and its neighbouring states on the east coast, Illinois (which includes Chicago) and its neighbouring states around the Great Lakes, and California and its neighbouring states on the west coast. The state of California is immensely wealthy.

The USA has a large agricultural industry producing a wide range of commodities of which cereals, cotton and tobacco are exported on a major scale. Not surprisingly, it has a very large food processing industry. It also has an extensive mining industry producing oil and gas, cereal, copper, iron, uranium and silver. The manufacturing industry is the world leader in many areas including steel, vehicles, aerospace, telecommunications, chemicals, electronics and consumer goods. Any importer looking for products should always look to see what is available from the USA and what is being developed.

The currency is the dollar (US$) which used to be regarded as the strongest currency in the world, but because of a large national debt, budget deficits and some loss of technical and managerial efficiency to countries such as Japan, its currency has been slowly losing its world domination and may be challenged by the single European Currency, the Euro. UK importers will probably find that suppliers want to be paid in dollars rather than in sterling.

Some very important international fairs are held in the USA, such as the one for textile machinery. Some UK importers will wish to attend such fairs in order to meet potential suppliers and to bring themselves up to date with any new products. Care should be taken in deciding which fairs to attend; it is important to ensure that the right suppliers will be exhibiting and not to be misled by the strong sales promotion of a fair. UK nationals visiting the USA do not need a visa if they are staying for less than 90 days and hold a return ticket. Other visitors should check the situation with their travel agent.

Information on USA exporters can be obtained from the US Embassy's Commercial Department in London who from time to time hold fairs at which UK buyers can meet visiting businesspeople. Many directories and other sources of information on American businesses can be found in the DTI's EMIC library in Victoria Street, London. UK buyers new to the American market should be selective and check up on potential suppliers, as in most product areas there are many from which to choose and some will not be reliable.

CANADA

Canada is the world's seventh largest exporter and importer and is thus a member of the G7 group of major industrial economies. It has immense natural resources and occupies a vast land area of which over 40 per cent is forest. It is a major exporter of grains, oil seeds and fish as well as many minerals. The largest economic sector is manufacturing, covering a whole range of activities. About 75 per cent of Canada's trade is with the USA and after that with Japan, the UK, Germany, Taiwan and France. Canada is a member of NAFTA and this is boosting its trade still further.

Canada is 4800 miles from east to west and has a good air, rail and road system in addition to extensive navigable waterways through rivers, canals and a vast number of lakes. The St Lawrence seaway is extensively used by shipping lines for moving goods, particularly between the Great Lakes and the Atlantic coast and beyond. The west coast is well served by shipping lines from ports such as Vancouver.

Although Canada is bilingual, ie English and French, the former is normally used in international business and UK importers should have no difficulty in negotiating purchases. The Canadian dollar (C$) is a strong currency and buyers may be able to get a better deal by buying in Canadian dollars rather than in pounds sterling. Information on Canadian exporters and their products can be obtained from the Commercial Section of the Canadian High Commission or the Canada-United Kingdom Chamber of Commerce in London.

MEXICO

Mexico is the fifteenth largest country in the world by area with a population of 84 million people. It is a member of NAFTA which is why it has been included in this chapter, although it is still in many ways a developing country. This new free trade area rivals the EU in population and net output.

The country consists of 31 states and a federal district. Over the past decade the country has been modernized, privatized and deregulated, but most of the investment has gone into the northern states which have borders with the USA. These industrial areas and those around Mexico City are responsible for much of the output of manufactured goods which constitute 80 per cent of the country's exports. Petroleum is still a major export (approximately 10 per cent of the whole) but other exports include automobiles, autoparts, cotton, coffee, tomatoes and other vegetables, shrimps, copper, silver, cattle, meat and petrochemicals. Mexico is the world's largest producer of silver and a leading producer of sulphur, lead and zinc. Major manufacturing sectors are food processing, electrical and electronic goods, textiles and apparel, wood, and metal furniture. Spain is the largest importer of Mexican goods, followed by France and Germany.

Tourism is the second largest source of foreign revenue in Mexico and an increasing number of UK agents are now offering Mexican holidays. The official language is Spanish but English is widely spoken.

The currency is the peso but because of inflation it has suffered against the dollar. It is probable that Mexican exporters will wish to be paid in US dollars until their currency has become much more stable.

Communications are good with all the main towns connected by air, road and rail. However, rail travel is rather slow. Parts of the country are underdeveloped and there are political and social problems which are only slowly being solved by more investment.

JAPAN

Japan is one of the strongest trading nations in the world, second only to the USA. It has a population of over 125 million people and a very modern economy. Culturally, it is very different from Europe and business discussions are generally very formal. In particular, there is no word for 'No' in Japanese and non-committal replies can be misinterpreted and confusing. Many Japanese speak English but an interpreter may be required.

The Japanese economy is very strong and while it has been through a long period of recession, it has still managed to maintain a large, positive balance in its international trade. The standards and technological achievements of the best companies are very high. The Japanese have very large trading companies which are responsible for most sales and distribution in the home market and overseas. Manufactured goods are responsible for most of their export earnings but gradually the Japanese are moving the manufacture of vehicles and electronic goods overseas to markets where manufacturers' costs are lower so they can protect their market share in trading areas such as the European single market.

UK importers will find it very easy to do business with the major Japanese exporting companies, although they may have to buy through their agents or from their stockists in the UK. Should they visit Japan, they should have no difficulty in travelling around as there is an outstandingly efficient rail system. Trains and hotels are expensive. Appointments must be made in advance and punctuality is essential. Politeness at all times is important and anger is not understood. A good stock of business cards is essential and the Japanese translation should be printed on the back. This can be easily arranged on arrival in the country. There are many conferences and exhibitions in Japan. Details about them can be obtained from the DTI's Export Services Directorate. Information on Japanese products and exporters can be obtained from JETRO (the Japan External Trade Organization) and the Japanese Chamber of Commerce and Industry in London.

AUSTRALIA

Australia has a very diverse economy and a standard of living comparable with Western Europe. It has a very strong agricultural base which still contributes 40 per cent of its export earnings, but its relative importance has fallen in recent years due to the exploitation of mineral deposits. Australia has vast reserves of coal, oil, natural gas, nickel, zircon, iron ore, bauxite and diamonds. Its main trading partner is Japan followed by the USA, New Zealand, China and the European Union countries, mainly the UK and Germany.

The population of Australia is heavily concentrated in the coastal regions as the interior is very arid. People rely on planes to get from place to place because of the large distances involved. Its major ports are fully capable of handling all its imports and exports. English is the normal language for use in business and socially, but within the country there are some minority communities that still retain their own languages. Air services between the UK and Australia are excellent. The currency is the Australian Dollar (A$) which is reasonably stable and freely exchangeable. UK importers visiting Australia should ensure that they deal only with reliable and reputable companies whose good quality and delivery performance is well known. New products such as wines have been making an increasing impact in the UK in addition to other agricultural products which are already known.

Information on Australian exporters and their products can be obtained from the Australian Trade Commission (Austrade) and the Australian-British Chamber of Commerce in London. The names and addresses of various other organizations who specialize in different aspects of Australian business can be found in the Business and Services telephone directory for the London postal area. One such body is the Australian Tourist Commission for those interested in offering holidays in Australia.

NEW ZEALAND

New Zealand is a small country consisting of two major islands, North Island and South Island, and some smaller islands. It has an English-speaking population of less than 4 million people. In the past the agricultural sector has been regarded as New Zealand's main industry but today it contributes less than 8 per cent to the GNP and it employs less than 10 per cent of the workforce. The country has significant natural resources of which natural gas and coal have been developed. In the last two decades New Zealand has established new enterprises based on its natural resources to replace the declining traditional industries such as textiles, agricultural machinery and fertilizers. New Zealand is a member of the Organization for Economic Cooperation and Development (OECD) which consists of the 24 most industrialized nations.

The currency is the New Zealand Dollar (NZ$) which is very stable partly because the country has very low inflation. Communications between the UK and New Zealand are excellent for both travellers and freight. The country has very good air, sea and road communications and hotel accommodation is excellent. Any UK importer visiting the country should experience no difficulties. Information on New Zealand exporters and their products can be obtained from the New Zealand Trade Development Board, the New Zealand-UK Chamber of Commerce and various specialist organizations such as the New Zealand Apple and Pear Marketing Board (UK) Ltd and the New Zealand Meat Producers Board. Travel agents in the UK are already very good at marketing holidays in New Zealand.

SOUTH AFRICA

South Africa is a country of some 35 million people, if the homelands are included. It is one of the world's largest economies and is dominant in the southern half of Africa. It has been through a difficult few years but provided it can maintain political stability under the new government, its future prospects are very good. The country has extensive mineral resources, except for oil, and the foundation of South Africa's economy is mining. It exports valuable minerals such as gold, diamonds, platinum, chromium, manganese and vanadium. Its agricultural industry is efficient and it is a successful exporter of fruit and wines. The largest sector of the economy is manufacturing. The metal industries produce steel, heavy engineering goods, production machinery and transport equipment. Advanced technological and service industries have been developed. Food processing and textile manufacturing are important. Light industries have also developed significantly.

Communications between the UK and South Africa by air and sea are excellent. Within the country there is a very good domestic air service between the main towns. Because of the distances involved, travel by road or rail is much slower. Hotel accommodation is very good. The language used in all international business is English, which is the most widely spoken language in South Africa.

The currency is the Rand (R) which, unfortunately, is a very weak currency – in part due to the very high levels of unemployment. A number of UK banks have branches in South Africa and a number of South African banks have branches in London so UK importers should have no problems in arranging payments.

There are many opportunities for UK importers in South Africa, not only for goods but also for services. Tourist agencies in the UK are promoting holidays in South Africa, and public relations and advertising companies are seeking opportunities to promote South African products and services. Information on South African companies can be obtained from the Commercial Section of the South African Embassy in London and from appropriate directories and trade magazines.

TURKEY

Turkey is included in this section because it is one of the world's 24 most industrialized countries and hence a member of the OECD. It has a population of about 40 million people who speak Turkish except for some of the Kurdish minority. It is essentially a Muslim state although there is a small Christian minority. Agriculture is still the most important sector with exports such as tobacco and cotton. Fruit, dried fruit and nuts are also major exports. There is an active mining sector producing copper, chromium, borax and, to a lesser extent, bauxite and coal. The manufacturing sector has grown over the years and is concentrated in textiles, iron and steel. Chemicals and light engineering have also been increasing in importance. Previously, Turkish exports were very much to Middle East countries but now they are directed at the European Union countries. It has close ties with Germany, partly because of the large number of Turkish migrants who work there. The USA is also an important export market for its products.

Communications between the UK and Turkey are by air, road, rail and sea and are efficient. A UK importer visiting the country will find that air and road travel between the major cities is better than rail. Although Turkey appears to be very bureaucratic, Turkish exporters do not seem to have any major problems, but care should be taken in selecting reliable exporters. Some of their major companies are represented in the UK. The currency is the Turkish Lira (TL) which is still subject to inflation so Turkish exporters will ask for payment in a hard currency. Information on Turkish exporters and their products can be obtained from the Commercial Section of the Turkish Embassy, the Turkish-British Chamber of Commerce and Industry and the Middle East Association, all in London.

HONG KONG AND SINGAPORE

These two countries have vibrant and developed economies and for many people they are still regarded as gateways to other countries in the region. Hong Kong has a population of about 6 million people and Singapore has about 3 million. Both occupy small land areas: Hong Kong 415 square miles and Singapore 242 square miles. They are both stable communities although control of Hong Kong has reverted to China.

The mainstay of the Hong Kong economy is the light manufacturing industry, financial services and shipping. The manufacturing sector includes thriving textile and consumer electronics industries. It is the leading world producer of children's toys. The currency is the Hong Kong Dollar (HK$) but it has suffered from inflation. Hong Kong is the world's eleventh largest trading economy and its major trading partner is China followed by Japan, Taiwan, the UK and the

USA. Its close association with the neighbouring Guangdong province of China, which has become very industrialized, makes it an important gateway for Chinese goods for those UK importers who do not wish to buy directly from China.

Singapore's prosperity rests on its entrepôt trade, shipbuilding and oil refining, electronics, banking and tourism. Like Hong Kong, it is a transshipment port for large container ships where cargo has to be split up into smaller consignments for other ports. High technology manufacturing, especially of computer and telecommunications equipment and financial services, has led to export growth. Singapore is also the most important telecommunications hub in South East Asia. The principal customers for Singapore's products and services are Japan, the USA and Malaysia.

Communications between the UK and Hong Kong and Singapore are excellent both by air and by sea. English is used in both countries in business and administration and UK importers should have no difficulty in doing business. The Hong Kong Trade Development Council and the Singapore Trade Development Board, both in London, can provide comprehensive information including catalogues of products offered by their exporters. No difficulties should be experienced in finding possible suppliers of a product or service, but the usual care must be taken in developing a trading relationship.

11

Rest of the World

The very varied markets in the rest of the world require a great understanding of the differences in language, culture, politics and religion. Although English is regarded as the language of international trade, many businesspeople do not speak it fluently and care must be taken to reach a proper understanding with suppliers. These are not, in many cases, such sophisticated international traders as those in developed countries. While there are risks in doing business in developed countries, they are likely to be greater in the developing countries: the political and commercial risks are very high and fraud is not uncommon, so great care must be taken in your choice of suppliers.

The single administrative document (SAD) is used by most countries in the rest of the world; however, other documents will often be required to enable your supplier to export the goods and for them to be imported into the EU, particularly if they are eligible for a preferential, ie lower, rate of duty.

The generalised system of preferences (GSP) scheme fixed for four years came into effect on 1 January 1995. It covers industrial products only, including textiles, while agricultural products are dealt with separately. The key feature of the scheme is that there are no tariff quotas and ceilings. The preferential rate is not universally nil and will particularly affect the less developed countries.

Information on licensing requirements for restricted goods is published in information for the importers, notice to importers or DTI press release notices. These can be obtained from the import licensing branch at Billingham and appear from time to time in the Thursday edition of Lloyds List; changes to EC regulations are published in information to importers notices. The community regimes cover three general areas:

- textiles and clothing
- iron and steel
- other products (for example, toys).

Importers must ensure that their goods are genuinely eligible for preferential rates of duty or they could suffer penalties. Detailed information on the new GSP is available from the DTI and the European Commission. Any importer wishing to know the duty position on any particular product should contact his local Excise and Customs Inland Advice Centre.

CHINA

The most important developing country, now that some of the Pacific Rim and Basin countries have become industrialized, is China, which is slowly establishing internationally agreed trading policies and which in due course will no doubt be accepted completely into GATT.

The vast Chinese economy with a population of over 1 billion people has grown rapidly, experiencing major economic growth in the 1980s and 1990s. Much of this growth has occurred in the coastal provinces and along the main rivers. One of the main areas of development has been in Guangdong province which surrounds Hong Kong. Considerable investments from Hong Kong have gone into this area and many products produced there can be obtained through Hong Kong.

China is one of the world's largest producers of rice and principal source of wheat, tobacco, soya beans, peanuts and cotton. Its mineral resources are among the richest in the world, particularly coal, crude oil, iron ore, tin, lead, bauxite (aluminium), tungsten, molybdenum, phosphates and manganese. It has developed heavy engineering and petrochemical industries. However, there has been a big shift in the past 15 years to light engineering industries. The petrochemical industry concentrates on producing fertilizers and synthetic fibres. In the consumer goods area the emphasis has been on producing textiles and clothing and these account for about 15 per cent of the gross industrial output.

Communications between the UK and various parts of China are not easy; normally you travel by air to Beijing, the capital, or to Hong Kong whence it is possible to travel by domestic airlines to various parts of China. The location of many factories in the coastal belts or along the main rivers means that there is no serious difficulty in shipping goods to the UK by sea. However, the sea voyage does take a few weeks. The currency is the Renminbi (RMB – the people's money), also known as the Yuan (Y), but payments are normally made in sterling or other hard currency. Visas are required by anyone who wishes to visit China. Information on Chinese export products and Chinese exporters can be obtained from the Chinese Chamber of Commerce UK and the China-Britain Trade Group in London.

EMERGING COUNTRIES IN THE FAR EAST

The emerging countries of the Far East include Indonesia, Malaysia, South Korea, Taiwan, Thailand and the Philippines. Products from these countries, such as cars, electronic equipment and textiles, are already on sale in UK shops and some of the major companies have started to invest in manufacturing or assembly units in the UK.

Indonesia is the largest of these countries, with a population of 160 million people. It has large reserves of oil and natural gas, which are the backbone of the economy, as well as mineral reserves of tin, bauxite, nickel, copper and gold. It is one of the world's leading producers of rubber and a major source of tea and coffee. The manufacturing industry has grown steadily. The Indonesia Trade Promotions Centre can provide information on exporters and their products.

Malaysia has a long history of trading relations with the UK and is well known for its exports of rubber, tea and palm oil. It is the world's largest producer of rubber. During the last decade it has been concentrating on developing a manufacturing industry based on its natural resources as well as in new product areas such as electronics, photographic and transport equipment, machinery, steel and textiles. Its cars, cameras and tropical fruits, eg pineapples, and rubber goods such as surgical gloves, are already widely seen in the UK market. UK importers should find very few difficulties in importing from Malaysia in view of the close ties between the two countries. The Malaysian Trade Commission can assist any UK importer looking for suppliers either by putting them in touch with producers in Malaysia or with UK agents of existing exporters.

South Korea is one of the so-called 'tiger' economies of the Pacific Rim and it is the world's twelfth largest trading nation. Its economic strength is based on shipbuilding, steel, consumer electronics and construction. The family-owned commercial groups, the *chaebol*, dominate the country. *Chaebol* companies that are well known outside Korea include Samsung, Hyundai, Lucky Goldstar and Daewoo. The country has a population of about 44 million people, most of whom live on the flat plain which occupies 30 per cent of the country. Communications between the UK and Korea's main ports, Pusan, Inchon (for Seoul, the capital), Kunsan and Makpo are good, as are air links between London and Seoul. The Korea Trade Centre in London can provide information on the *chaebol* companies' agents in the UK as well as the names of other Korean exporters and their products.

Taiwan, after phenomenal growth, is now among the top 20 trading nations in the world. Its low overheads and low labour costs have contributed to its exceptional growth. It is an island country with a population of about 21 million people and, although the official language is Mandarin, most businesspeople speak English. The principal industries in Taiwan are textiles, shipbuilding, metals, plywood, furniture, and petrochemicals. The financial services, and electronics withinformation technology, are the new industries being developed.

Taiwan is the leading 'tiger' economy of the Pacific Basin. Its main trading partners are Japan, Germany, Australia, mainland China and Saudi Arabia. Communications by air between the capital, Taipei, and London are good for travellers, and for freight by sea between Taiwan and the UK. Most Taiwan exporters will require payment in US dollars. There is a strong exchange control system. Information on Taiwan exports can be obtained from the Taiwan Trade Centre in London and the Taiwan External Trade Development Council in Taipei.

Thailand is another relatively prosperous country in the Far East. It has always had a strong agricultural base and is the world's leading exporter of rice, besides which it exports sugar, cassava, maize, rubber, cotton and tobacco. Industrially, it has developed cement manufacturing, electronics, jewellery, sugar and oil refining. In the service sector tourism is very important and many UK travel agents offer holidays in Thailand. The Economics Section of the Thai Embassy can provide information on Thai exporters.

The Philippines is another country showing good economic growth. While it is still basically agricultural, the government has made special efforts to encourage the manufacture of goods for export. Products now seen in world markets include semi-conductors, garments, furniture, giftware and food products. Its major trading partners include the USA, the UK and the Netherlands. The Embassy's Trade and Investment Office can provide information on exporters.

INDIAN SUB-CONTINENT

The countries of the Indian sub-continent, Pakistan, Bangladesh and Sri Lanka, have had a long trading relationship with the UK. They are all members of the British Commonwealth and, because of their history, have acquired many UK customs. English is the business language of the sub-continent. They are all heavily populated countries and poverty is widespread. All the countries have essentially rural populations but have been following policies of industrialization.

India has a well-developed industrial economy which has invested in advanced technology. In the last two decades it has expanded greatly in heavy engineering, notably transport equipment, iron and steel, chemicals and electronics. It has a long-established textile industry although much of it is still a cottage industry and quality is unreliable. The textile industry is also very important in Pakistan, Bangladesh and Sri Lanka and is a useful export earner in all these countries. India has been developing high technology industries, eg digital communications and space research.

Pakistan has been developing its chemical industry, notably for the manufacture of synthetic fibres to support its textile industry which is strongly based on home-grown cotton. The country has a well-established food processing and construction industry. Light industries, such as the manufacture of plastic products, have also become well established. In addition to textiles, Pakistan also exports other consumer goods such as leather products.

India, Bangladesh and Sri Lanka are major sources of tea. Jute is also a very important crop for Bangladesh. The jute-related industries, textiles, chemicals and sugar are important manufacturing industries. Jute products are exported to the UK with other products. The USA is Bangladesh's largest market followed by Italy, Japan, Singapore and the UK.

Sri Lanka is an island with a population of 18 million people. It is predominantly an agricultural economy. The main export crops are tea, rubber and coconuts but tropical fruits such as pineapples are of increasing importance. The main industrial sectors are mining and manufacturing. The mining and export of gemstones is very important to the economy. A textile industry has been developed mainly to capture exports. British textile companies have been encouraged to invest in Sri Lanka because of the low labour costs. The UK is the third largest export market for Sri Lankan goods.

Information on exporters from these countries can be obtained from the High Commissions for India, Pakistan, Bangladesh and Sri Lanka, all in London.

SOUTH AMERICA

The South American countries have always been of importance to the UK and are probably most associated with coffee from Brazil, meat from Argentina and bananas from various parts of the West Indies and Ecuador (the world's largest producer of bananas). Although most of the countries have great potential, political or economic instability coupled with inflation have prevented the full development of their potential.

Brazil is the largest country on the continent with a population of about 155 million people, mainly Portuguese speaking. It covers almost half of South America and is the fifth largest country in the world. Its economic output is the tenth highest. Brazil is the world's second largest exporter of agricultural products, mainly coffee, cocoa, sugar, soya beans, orange juice, beef and poultry. It also produces sisal, tobacco, maize and cotton and has a large forestry industry. Industrial sectors include machinery, electrical goods, construction materials, rubber, chemicals and vehicles. The country has vast mineral reserves and is one of the world's biggest exporters of iron ore. Brazil has a healthy trade surplus but still has enormous overseas debts and has suffered from hyper-inflation. The principal trading partners are the USA, Japan, Germany and other countries in the South American trading bloc.

Information on Brazilian exporters and their products can be obtained from the Brazilian Trade Centre, the Brazilian Chamber of Commerce and Economic Affairs in Great Britain, and the Latin American Trade Advisory Group (LATAG) at Canning House in London. The latter has a very good library and a number of activities to promote trade and good relationships with South American countries.

Argentina is the second largest country in South America with a population of about 33 million Spanish-speaking people. It is rich in natural resources and has a large and profitable agricultural sector. It is a major exporter of wheat and produces maize, oilseeds, sorghum, soya beans and sugar. Meat is still produced in large quantities but is not now such an important export. The industrial sector has been protected and so has been relatively inefficient. However, Argentina does export textiles, some metals and chemical products. Brazil is its largest trading partner but the USA, Japan, the CIS (mostly former USSR states) and the European Union countries are also important. Argentina has suffered from the effects of hyper-inflation and has a massive foreign debt.   Information on Argentina's exporters and their products can be obtained from their UK Embassy's Commercial Department and from the Canning House library at LATAG in London.

Chile, with a population of about 14 million people, is one of the strongest economies in South America. Its people are Spanish speaking but many also speak English. The country is still very dependent on its agricultural, horticultural and mining industries, although it has well-developed industrial and service sectors. Its main exports are metals, ores, wood, fruit and fish. It has a large surplus of fruit and vegetables which it exports to North America and Europe. The UK has a long history of good trading relationships with Chile and there are established UK importers of products from that country.

The two main oil and gas producing countries in South America are *Venezuela* and *Colombia*. The former is the wealthiest country on the continent. It has the second largest known oil reserve in the world (after Saudi Arabia). The agricultural industry is still very important and dairy and beef products are major export earners. Venezuela has a population of about 12 million compared with Colombia's population of about 33 million.

Colombia is one of South America's strongest economies and is set to become even stronger when its oil and gas reserves have been more fully developed. Currently, agriculture accounts for about 75 per cent of the country's export earnings. Coffee, sugar, bananas, cut flowers and cotton are all exported. Colombia also exports gemstones, textiles, leather goods, metal products, chemicals, pharmaceuticals and cement. The language is primarily Spanish but some English is spoken. A tourist industry is being developed which will provide opportunities for UK travel agents. It has large reserves of good, open cast coal which are also being developed and exported to the UK among other countries. Colombia is important for both UK importers and exporters as long as it can remain politically stable and operate sensible economic policies. It is likely to become a very wealthy country. The Colombian Embassy and the Canning House LATAG services can provide information on Colombian exporters.

Other South American countries such as Ecuador, Bolivia, Peru, Uruguay and Guyana all have good trading relationships with the UK.

EASTERN EUROPE

The Eastern European countries have become much more important to UK importers following the break-up of the Communist bloc. Poland, Hungary, the Czech Republic and the Slovak Republic are all looking to the West to increase their international trade, having been very dependent on the Soviet bloc. They would like to join the EU but are unlikely to be admitted to full membership before the next century. Poland already has associate membership and the others will probably gain it in the next few years. Poland is the UK's major trading partner among these four countries. Agriculture plays an important role in all of them. Poland's main industries are shipbuilding, textiles, steel, cement, chemicals and foodstuffs. Hungary's industries are mainly involved in chemicals, plastics, pharmaceuticals, fertilizers, computers, telecommunications, mining, construction, engineering and aluminium production. Hungary exports a wide range of agricultural and horticultural products such as maize, wheat, sugar beet, potatoes, fruit and vegetables and livestock. Information on trading with these countries, and others such as Bulgaria and Romania, can be obtained from the East European Trade Council and the various countries' embassies.

COMMONWEALTH OF INDEPENDENT STATES

The CIS comprises most of the former members of the USSR. The important countries in the west are Russia, Belarus and the Ukraine. All are characterized by economic and, to a varying extent, political instability. The CIS occupies one-sixth of the land area in the world and has a population of about 280 million. The states have an enormous abundance of natural resources including almost every known mineral and energy resource based on indigenous oil, gas, coal, hydroelectric power and nuclear plants. There are vast areas of fertile land, forest and fresh water. The CIS has a poor agriculture system and an inadequate infrastructure. Industry is mainly concentrated in the heavy industry sector, especially steel, heavy engineering and chemicals.

Purchasing from the countries in this group is at present fraught with problems and anyone interested in any of their products should attempt to find established and reliable traders in the UK or in other European Union countries. Information on the individual states' exporters and their products can be sought from their individual embassies or representatives in London. Travel to these countries and within them is not easy and is generally by air. As far as possible business should be conducted in the main cities.

MEDITERRANEAN COUNTRIES OUTSIDE THE EU

Turkey has already been mentioned (p 83), but Morocco, Tunisia, Algeria, Libya, Egypt, Israel, Syria, Lebanon and the former Yugoslavia can all be considered as being in the group. All these countries trade with each other and with other countries around the Mediterranean as well as with those with whom they have land borders. They are particularly keen to develop trade with the EU countries as they recognize the potential of the single market.

The UK and *Israel*, in particular, have a strong trading relationship. This is partly historical and partly because Israel has a diverse and sophisticated manufacturing economy. Citrus fruits are a significant export but industrial exports are much more important. The industrial sector is concentrated in engineering, aircraft, electronics, chemicals, construction materials, textiles and food processing. Tourism is also quite important and growing. Information on Israel's exporters can be obtained from the Embassy of Israel.

Egypt, a country of about 54 million people, also has good trading relationships with the UK. Its major industries are textiles, fertilizers, cement and rubber products. In addition, it has a major steelworks, several vehicle assembly plants and a light engineering sector. It has a useful level of oil production, mainly for its own use, and a significant tourist industry. In the past it has tended to trade with other Arab countries and the former Soviet Union and Eastern Europe; however, its trade is now very much more directed to the EU countries. Information on Egypt's exports and its exporters can be obtained from the Embassy of the Arab Republic of Egypt and the Egyptian-British Chamber of Commerce.

Morocco, with a population of about 26 million, is situated at the westernmost end of the Mediterranean. The official language is Arabic but French is widely spoken except in the northern part of the country where Spanish is predominant. Its main trading partners are France and Spain but the UK is still significant. Morocco is essentially an agricultural country producing cereals, citrus fruits and vegetables, some for export. It is the world's largest producer and exporter of phosphate rock. The Embassy of the Kingdom of Morocco can provide information on Moroccan exporters and their goods.

Among the other countries in this section, Algeria, Libya and Syria have economies very dependent on their oil production and trading. Tunisia is small but has a growing tourist industry and the former Yugoslavia and Lebanon are still war torn, although the latter is recovering.

MIDDLE EAST

The main Middle East countries are Saudi Arabia, Iran and Iraq which, like other countries in the region, have economies dependent to varying extents on their production of oil and natural gas. Almost all Saudi Arabia's exports are oil, natural gas and products derived from them. However, like Iraq, they are also significant producers and exporters of dates. The effects of war and its after-effects, ie the United Nations' embargo on Iraq, have almost brought Iraq's exports to a halt. Iran has also been affected by war and an inefficient government, but it is trying to improve its agricultural production and light industry sector, and there has been some recovery in its oil exports.

SUB-SAHARAN AFRICA

South Africa has been reviewed in Chapter 10. The remaining countries in Africa south of the Sahara desert depend essentially on their agricultural and mining industries. Some agricultural products, such as cocoa and coffee, are exported in significant quantities. A few are producers of oil and natural gas. All tend to be politically and economically unstable and there are often risks in doing business with them. Payments should preferably be on a CIF UK port basis so that you can be confident the goods have actually arrived in the UK before you pay for them.

The *Ivory Coast* (Côte d'Ivoire) is an important exporter of cocoa, coffee and cotton and, to a lesser extent, timber and fruit. It has established light industries producing textiles, chemicals and sugar, mainly for export. The country has established trading patterns with some EU countries, particularly the Netherlands. *Ghana* is also a significant exporter of cocoa and timber and the UK is its largest trading partner.

Nigeria has a population of about 90 million people and in these terms is the largest country in Africa. It has vast oil and natural gas reserves and the sale of oil products accounts for 90 per cent of its foreign earnings. It has a large but inefficient agricultural industry which still exports cash crops such as groundnuts, cocoa and palm oil. Many major manufacturing industries, such as the manufacture of textiles, have been established and are responsible for some exports, mainly to neighbouring countries.

Kenya is one of Africa's stronger economies. It is primarily an agricultural country exporting mainly coffee and tea but also vegetables and flowers. It has a light industry including several textile mills. The UK is a major trading partner along with Germany. Neighbouring *Tanzania* is a mainly agricultural country exporting cotton, coffee, tea, tobacco and cashew nuts. It has a small manufacturing industry processing sugar and making textiles, beer and cigarettes.

Zimbabwe is also a strong agricultural country which exports cash crops such as tobacco, sugar, coffee, cotton, tea, groundnuts and beef. The mining industry is important and in comparison with its northern neighbours its manufacturing industry is well developed. Its main export markets are Germany, Japan, the UK and the USA. Zimbabwe is a member of the Lomé, Convention which governs trade between the EU and the African Caribbean and Pacific (ACP) countries. It is one of the better countries with which UK importers can do business, although it has serious economic problems with a substantial overseas debt.

In general, when importing from these African countries it is important to visit them frequently or to have an agent to look after your interests in each country in which you are involved. Those new or relatively new to importing will probably find it advisable to buy from established importers from these countries. Such traders are most likely to be found in the UK, Germany, the Netherlands and France.

CENTRAL AFRICA

Communications between the UK and some of the less developed countries are not good, for example those in Central Africa. This also applies to some parts of those countries such as Zaire, which do not have good internal communications. In general, new UK importers will find it easier to obtain goods from existing UK importers who have already overcome any transport or other problems.

12

Further Information

GLOSSARY

ad valorem duty Duty based on a percentage of the cargo value.

aircraft manifest List of individual consignments on an aircraft.

air waybill Air freight consignment document made out by, or on behalf of, the shipper. It is a document of title.

aligned forms Series of forms designed so that information appears on each form in the pack as required by recipients.

arbitration Method of settling disputes which is usually binding on the parties involved. Many international trade contracts contain arbitration clauses stipulating the method of arbitration.

avalize To guarantee payment by a bank of a bill of exchange.

banker's draft A draft drawn by one bank on another bank in favour of a third party. Drafts should comply with the rules for cheques in the country in which they are payable.

bill of exchange An unconditional order in writing, addressed by one party or person to another, signed by the party giving it, requiring the party to whom it is addressed to pay on demand or at a fixed or determinable future time a sum of money to, or to the order of, a specified party or the bearer.

bill of lading A receipt of goods placed on board a ship, signed by the person or agent who contracts to carry them. It states the terms on which the goods are carried and is a current document of title.

carnet A document usually obtained from Chambers of Commerce which allows the temporary importation without payment of duty of commercial samples, exhibition materials and similar goods.

certificate of origin A document identifying the goods shipped and expressly stating where the goods were manufactured, eg originated. They are usually certified by Chambers of Commerce.

clean bill of lading A bill of lading with no additional clauses declaring a defective state of the goods or packaging.

consignment note A document which usually states the terms under which goods are carried. It normally accompanies the goods throughout transit.

consolidation The system of sending a number of consignments from various consignees to various consignors as one overall consignment. It is also known as groupage.

customs entry The form on which the importer gives details of the goods for customs clearance.

del credere The agent's guarantee to his principal for the solvency of the parties to whom he makes sales. It is included in agency agreements when required.

demurrage The money paid by the shipper or the seller for delays in loading, discharge or occupying space at a port or warehouse beyond a specified period. It usually arises from customs clearance delays.

documentary collection The exporter's bank sends the appropriate documents, including that of title, to the importer's bank. The importer usually receives the documents in exchange for payment or acceptance of a term bill of exchange.

documentary letter of credit Document whereby, at the buyer's request, his bank authorizes the exporter to draw payment by a specified date of a particular shipment against the presentation of accurate and detailed documents in accordance with the terms of credit.

exchange rate Price of one currency in terms of another.

ex-works See page 32.

factor A company which administers the sales ledger, pays the exporter and collects payment from the importer or his agent/bank.

force majeure A clause limiting the responsibilities of suppliers and shippers under certain circumstances. Usually this clause is included in the contract conditions.

forfeiter The forfeiting company purchases for cash a seller's receivables. The seller receives payment from the forfeiter and loses his right to the future payment. The forfeiter collects payment from the buyer or his agent/bank.

forwarding agent The party responsible for the arrangements for importing/exporting cargo. Usually described as a freight forwarder.

groupage System of sending various packages from different consignees under one agent to a common destination. It is also known as consolidation.

indemnity Compensation for loss, damage or injury.

insurance certificate A certificate that is proof that insurance for a particular shipment has been arranged.

intermodal Carriage by various means of transport, eg air, sea, road and rail.

letter of indemnity A document indemnifying the agent or shipper from any risk or claims that may arise through the use of an incorrect 'clean' bill of lading.

manifest List of cargo on board a ship.

market price The price at which a product would sell if sold on the open market.

negotiable bill of lading A bill of lading that can be transferred or endorsed.

pre-entry The process of lodging documents with customs prior to the shipment or arrival of goods.

revolving credits A system whereby the importer arranges with his bank for a certain sum to be available so that payment can be made for each shipment under a series of shipments usually under one contract.

sea waybill A non-negotiable document (that lists the goods) which is evidence of a contract for the carriage of goods by sea.

shipping documents Documents that enable shipments to be sent or received.

transshipment The process of transferring cargo from one transport mode to another.

wharfage The fees paid for using a wharf or accommodation at a wharf.

The following draft agreements have been contributed by:

Melanie Rowlands of Laytons Solicitors for International Trade whose address is Carmelite, 50 Victoria Embankment, Blackfriars, London EC4Y 0LS, Tel: 0171 842 8000, Fax: 0171 842 8080; and

Rebecca Attree, MIEx, Solicitor and Chairman of the London and Home Counties Branch of the Institute of Export. Address: 110 Cambridge Street, London SW1V 4QF, Tel: 0171 6306019, Fax 0171 630 8681.

DRAFT AGENCY AGREEMENT

THIS AGREEMENT is made the   day of   199
BETWEEN

(1)   [PRINCIPAL] [a company] [incorporated in England and Wales]
       [with registered number [   ] having its registered office
       at [   ]] ("the Principal"); and
(2)   [AGENT] [a company] [incorporated in England and Wales] [with
       registered number [   ] having its registered office at
       [   ]] ("the Agent")*

NOW IT IS HEREBY AGREED as follows:

1.   DEFINITIONS

1.1   In this Agreement including its Schedules:

"the Commencement Date"   -   is [   ];

"Net Invoice Price"   -   means the price actually charged
                            by the Principal to the customer
                            disregarding any transport and
                            insurance charges and any Value
                            Added Tax and other sales tax,
                            duties, tariffs or levies;

"the Products"   -   are the products listed in
                       Schedule 1;

"Quarter"   -   is a three-month period ending
                  on either 31st March, 30th June,
                  30th September or 31st
                  December;

"Terms and Conditions"   -   means the standard terms and
                               conditions of sale of the Principal as
                               notified from time to time by the
                               Principal to the Agent;

"the Territory"   -   is [   ] delineated in red
                        on the map in Schedule 2

1.2   References to clauses, sub-clauses, paragraphs and Schedules are refer-
       ences to the same in this Agreement
1.3   Clause headings shall be ignored in interpretation

2.   APPOINTMENT

**2.1   Appointment: The Principal hereby appoints the Agent as its [sole]
       [exclusive] agent for the marketing and sale of the Products in the
       Territory on the terms and conditions set out in this Agreement and the
       Agent accepts such appointment

---

*Parties: These will need careful amendment in the case of non-corporate par-
             ties and where either party is based overseas.
**2.1   A choice needs to be made between appointing a "sole" and an
            "exclusive" agent. By appointing a "sole" agent the principal is itself
            able to sell products in the territory but may not appoint another
            agent in the territory and the "not" in 2.4 should be deleted. By
            appointing an "exclusive" agent the principal is precluded from
            itself selling the products in the territory (the "not" in 2.4 should
            remain) and from appointing other agents or distributors to do so.
            Sub-clause 2.2. is optional but recommended for clarity.

[2.2 Other Agents or Distributors: The Principal shall not during the continuance of this Agreement appoint any other person, firm or company as the Principal's agent or distributor for the marketing and/or sale of the Products in the Territory]

2.3 No Sales by Agent Outside the Territory: The Agent shall not without the Principal's prior written consent solicit or accept any orders for the Products from any person outside the Territory or from any person in the Territory if the Agent knows or has reason to believe that the Products concerned will be resold outside the Territory

2.4 Direct Sales: The Principal shall [not] be entitled to make sales of the Products direct to customers in the Territory

3. PRINCIPAL'S RIGHTS AND OBLIGATIONS

3. The Principal shall:

(a) supply to the Agent a sufficient quantity of sales literature, samples and other promotional material, the Terms and Conditions and other information necessary for the satisfaction and performance of this Agreement;

(b) supply to the Agent the price list for the Products and inform the Agent of any price changes and where appropriate any changes to the Products or specifications of particular Products;

(c) be entitled from time to time to add to or withdraw items from the Products and to add additional area to or withdraw area from the Territory [upon giving to the Agent not less that one month's written notice at any time];*

(d) be entitled to accept or reject any order for the Products in the Territory whether such order has been notified by the Agent or otherwise

4. AGENT'S DUTIES

4.1 Duties: The Agent shall:

(a) use its best efforts to promote and obtain the maximum sales of the Products in the Territory;

(b) carry out such customer and end-user training programmes as the Principal may from time to time specify;

(c) provide such liaison and support services as the Principal may reasonably request;

(d) at its own expense, obtain and retain all applicable permissions, consents and licences necessary or advisable for the conduct of the business under this Agreement;

(e) inform the Principal promptly of any matters which may assist it in assessing the market for Products and similar products to the Products in the Territory;

(f) attend at its own expense such events as are agreed or necessary to promote properly the Products;

(g) not do anything that may prevent the sale or interfere with the development of sales of the Products in the Territory and without limitation not be concerned or interested directly or indirectly in the manufacture, sale, promotion, marketing or importation into the Territory of products which compete with the Products;

---

*3(c)   This is unlikely to be enforceable in respect of major alterations to the products and/or the territory.

(h)   promptly refer to the Principal all enquiries concerning the Products from customers and prospective customers both within and outside the Territory together with such details of such customers and prospective customers as the Principal shall reasonably require and promptly forward to the Principal all orders, requests and quotations it receives for the Products or products similar to the Products;

(i)   not hold itself out or permit any person to hold it out as being autho-rised to bind the Principal in any way and/or not do any act which might reasonably create the impression that it is so authorised;

(j)   promptly inform the Principal of:
(i) any complaint or after-sales enquiry concerning the Products which is received by the Agent
(ii) any matters likely to be relevant in relation to the manufacture, sale, use or development of the Products within or outside the Territory;

(k)   take all steps to ensure customers are creditworthy and promptly notify the Principal if the Agent has reasonable grounds to believe any customer is not creditworthy and shall not solicit orders from any such customer or any customer notified to the Agent which the Principal has reasonable grounds for believing is not creditworthy;

(l)   ensure sales of the Products will be in the Principal's sole name and solely upon the Terms and Conditions or such other terms as to price, specification, delivery or otherwise as the Principal notifies the Agent and/or customer for each particular order or quotation and the Agent shall not make or give any promises, warranties, guarantees or repre-sentations concerning the Products other than those contained in the Terms and Conditions;

(m)   forthwith remit all monies received by him on behalf of the Principal into an account (details of which the Principal shall notify in writing) and notify the Principal of any sums paid into such account from time to time

4.2   Warranty: The Agent warrants that its services and those carried out on its behalf under this Agreement will be carried out with reasonable skill and care and indemnifies and keeps the Principal indemnified for and against all proceedings, costs (including legal costs on an indem-nity basis), liabilities, injury, loss or damage arising from breach of this warranty or from its acts or omissions under this Agreement

5.   COMMISSION

5.1   Amount: In consideration of the obligations undertaken by the Agent hereunder the Principal shall pay to the Agent commission equal to [   ] per cent [%] of the Net Invoice Price of all Products which at any time during the continuance of this Agreement are sold by the Principal in the Territory to customers introduced at any time during the continuance of this Agreement by the Agent and where Value Added Tax is payable it shall be paid on all payments at the rate in force from time to time

5.2   Payment: The Principal shall within [seven] days after the end of each Quarter send to the Agent a statement showing the aggregate Net Invoice Price of the Products sold in the Territory by the Principal dur-ing the preceding Quarter together with a statement of the commission to which the Agent is entitled and upon receipt of such statement the Agent will send to the Principal an invoice in respect of such commission

5.3 Repayment and Deduction: There may be deducted from commission payable under sub-clause 5.1 any commission which would otherwise be payable in respect of a sale of Products in the Territory if payment for such Products is not made in full within [ninety] days of when it is payable and any commission overpaid in this respect shall be promptly repaid by the Agent to the Principal

5.4 Set-off: The Principal may set off against monies it owes to the Agent any monies the Agent owes to the Principal howsoever arising

6. INTELLECTUAL PROPERTY AND CONFIDENTIAL INFORMATION

6.1 Limitation: Nothing in this appointment confers upon the Agent any right, title or interest in the Principal's name or any trade marks, copyright, goodwill, patent, design, know-how or other similar or analogous property or rights from time to time of the Principal or any third party and the right to use such intellectual property is granted only to the extent that the Principal is able to do so without endangering the validity of any registration or right to apply for any registration

6.2 Notice of Infringement: The Agent shall promptly inform the Principal of any infringement or suspected infringement of any intellectual property rights which are the property of or used by the Principal of which it becomes aware and will assist the Principal (at the Principal's expense) to take any such action as is necessary in the Principal's view to defend its rights in the Territory

6.3 Confidence: The Agent will not disclose or use (other than as properly required by this appointment) any confidential information received or obtained by it concerning the Principal's busness or products and will use its best endeavours to keep such information confidential

7. DURATION AND TERMINATION

7.1 Term: This Agreement and the appointment hereunder shall commence on the Commencement Date and shall continue unless terminated by written notice by either party to the other such notice expiring at any time being not less than one month if expiring during the first year after the Commencement Date, not less than two months if expiring during the second year after the Commencement Date and not less than three months if expiring during the third and subsequent years after the Commencement Date

7.2 Early Termination by Either Party: Either party may at any time terminate this appointment forthwith by written notice to the other if:

(a) the other is in breach of any of the provisions of this appointment and the breach is either incapable of remedy or if it is capable of remedy the other fails to cure it within thirty days of being required by written notice to do so; or

(b) the other becomes insolvent or there is commenced by or against it any procedure which may lead to its liquidation, dissolution, bankruptcy, protection from its creditors or any similar or analogous process under the laws or statutes of any applicable country or state; or

(c) save as provided by clause 11 the other ceases to do business at any time for thirty or more consecutive business days

7.3   <u>Early Termination by the Principal</u>: The Principal may at any time terminate this appointment forthwith by notice in writing if at any time there is a material change in the management, ownership or control (where the Agent is a body corporate as defined in Section 840 of the Income and Corporation Taxes Act 1988) of the Agent

7.4   <u>Accrued Rights</u>: Termination for any reason will be without prejudice to any rights and obligations which have accrued prior thereto and to any provision of this appointment intended to take effect upon or continue in effect after termination

8.   <u>EFFECT OF TERMINATION</u>

8.1   <u>Return of Property</u>: Forthwith upon the Principal's request after termination of this appointment the Agent at its own expense shall return to the Principal in good order all samples, documents and other items of any nature whatsoever belonging to the Principal in the Agent's possession or control together with any copies, notices and memoranda of the same

8.2   <u>Cessation of Use of Name and Trade Marks</u>: Upon termination of this appointment the Agent shall have no further rights to use the Principal's intellectual property or the Principal's name or any other names or trade marks of the Principal or associated with the Products in any way whatsoever and the Agent shall sign such cessation of use or other documents as the Principal shall require in this respect

8.3   <u>Licences and Approvals</u>: Any permissions, consents, technical application or import licences and/or sale approvals obtained by the agent relating to the Products, their distribution and/or sale shall be the property of the Principal and upon termination of this appointment the Agent shall take all steps which the Principal reasonably requires to transfer such licences or approvals and related documentation to the Principal or any other person nominated by it

[9.   <u>TERMINATION PAYMENT</u>

9.1   <u>Entitlement</u>: Any termination payment claimed by the Agent hereunder shall be by way of [an indemnity] [compensation for damage and the Agent shall have no claim for loss of agency rights, goodwill or other such loss or any damages whatsoever other than a claim (if any) in accordance with this clause]*

9.2   <u>Amount</u>: The amount (if any) of termination payment to be paid to the Agent shall be calculated in accordance with the Commercial Agents (Council Directive) Regulations 1993 (as amended, modified or replaced from time to time)]

10.   <u>COVENANTS</u>

10.   The Agent undertakes that it shall not directly by itself or through its agents, employees or otherwise during the term of this Agreement

---

*9.1   If the agent operates in the United Kingdom the Commercial Agents (Council Directive) Regulations 1993 (SI 1993 No 3053) will probably apply and the agent will be entitled to a termination payment. The choice between an indemnity or compensation should be made and which of the two is most favourable to the agent will depend on the circumstances of the particular case. By Regulation 17(5) the grant of an indemnity does not preclude a right to damages.

and for a period of two years after the date of expiry or termination of this Agreement solicit, seek to solicit or enter into contracts with customers of the Principal in the Territory in respect of the Products or products of the same or similar kind from time to time included in this appointment

11. FORCE MAJEURE
11. Neither party shall be liable for any failure to perform properly under this Agreement if the reason for such failure is a result of an Act of God, act of government authorities or other incidents which are beyond the reasonable control of the defaulting party

12. GENERAL
12.1 No Partnership: Nothing in this Agreement shall create or be deemed to create a partnership or the relationship of employer and employee between the parties
12.2 Laws: This appointment shall be governed and construed in all respects in accordance with the laws of [England] and the parties irrevocably submit to the non-exclusive jurisdiction of the courts of [England and Wales]*
12.3 Sole Agreement: This appointment replaces all previous appointments or arrangements between the Principal and the Agent and constitutes the sole and entire agreement in that respect and the Agent has not relied upon any representation by the Principal inducing it to enter into this appointment
12.4 Notices: Any notice under this appointment must be given in writing and will be deemed to have been given properly by either party:
(a) if sent by registered post to the other at the address given above (or any other address from time to time notified to the other in writing) [seven days] after the date of its proper posting;
(b) if sent by effective facsimile or telex transmission upon the business day following the date of transmission in each case to such number notified to the other. Any such transmission shall be confirmed in writing sent by post forthwith
12.5 Non-Assignment: This Agreement is personal to the Agent who shall not without the prior written consent of the Principal mortgage, charge, assign or sub-contract all or any part of its interest hereunder
12.6 The Agent for Service: The Agent hereby appoints [full name and address] as its agent for service of any notice, demand or claim arising from the terms of this Agreement and for the service of any legal proceedings whether originating from a court arbitral or other institution or otherwise]**
12.7 Severance: If any provision of this Agreement is held by any court or other competent authority to be void or unenforceable in whole or in part this Agreement shall continue to be valid as to the other provisions thereto and the remainder of the affected provision

---

*12.2   A chosen law will not necessarily govern all matters arising from the agency agreement due to complex rules of private international law.
**12.6   In the case of an overseas agent the agent should appoint an agent for service of legal proceedings in England and Wales.

12.8   <u>Version</u>: The English language version of this Agreement shall be the definitive version and any translation of it shall be available for ease of reference only

IN WITNESS whereof the parties hereto have executed this Agreement the day and year first before written

SCHEDULE 1
The Products

The Products are the Products of the Principal listed below:

Name/Description   Model/Type Number

SCHEDULE 2
The Territory

SIGNED by   )*
[   ]   )
for and on behalf of   )
THE PRINCIPAL in the   )
presence of:)

Witness Name Address and Occupation:

SIGNED by   )
[   ]   )
for and on behalf of   )
THE AGENT in the   )
presence of:)

Witness Name Address and Occupation:

IMPORTANT: This model agreement provides an outline of the types of clauses frequently incorporated in an agency agreement. Specific legal advice should be sought on the particular facts before entering into such an agreement.

---

*   Execution Clauses: if either of the parties is incorporated or resident overseas, it is important to check that their execution of the agreement complies with the legal requirements for signature of the jurisdiction where they are incorporated or resident.

DRAFT DISTRIBUTION AGREEMENT

THIS AGREEMENT is made the   day of   199
BETWEEN

(1)   [PRINCIPAL] a [company] [incorporated in England and Wales]
        [with registered number [   ] having its registered office at
        [   ]] ("the Principal"); and
(2)   [DISTRIBUTOR] a [company] [incorporated in England and Wales]
        with registered number [   ] having its registered office at
        [   ]] ("the Distributor")*

NOW IT IS HEREBY AGREED as follows:

1.   DEFINITIONS
1.1   Definitions: In this agreement:

"the Commencement Date"   -   is [   ];
"Contract Period"   -   is the Initial Period and after that
                                    each year ending on the anniver-
                                    sary of the expiry of the Initial
                                    Period;
"Distributor List Price"   -   is the ex-works price for a product
                                    specified in the most recent
                                    Distributor price list from time to
                                    time published by the Principal;
"in Products"   -   are the products listed in Schedule
                                    1;
"the Territory"   -   is [   ] delineated in red
                                    on the map at Schedule 2

1.2   References to clauses, sub-clauses and Schedules are references to the
same in this Agreement
1.3   Clause headings shall be ignored in interpretation

2.   APPOINTMENT
**2.1   Rights: the Principal hereby grants to the Distributor the [sole] [exclu-
sive] right to distribute and sell the Products under the Principal's
name in the Territory on the terms and conditions set out in this
Agreement. [For the avoidance of doubt however the Principal shall
itself be free to manufacture and/or distribute and sell without restric-
tion any of the Products within or to any person within or for use
within the Territory]
2.2   Territory and Products: The Principal shall be entitled from time to

---

*Parties: These will need careful amendment in the case of non-corporate par-
              ties and where either party is operating from overseas.
**2.1   A choice needs to be made between appointing a "sole" and an
              "exclusive" distributor. By appointing a "sole" distributor the princi-
              pal is itself able to sell products in the territory but may not appoint
              another distributor in the territory (the second section should there-
              fore be retained). By appointing an "exclusive" distributor the prin-
              cipal is precluded from selling the products in the territory and from
              appointing other distributors to do so (and the second sentence
              should therefore be deleted).

time to add to or withdraw items from the Products and to add additional area or to withdraw area from the Territory [upon giving the Distributor not less than one month's written notice at any time]***

3. TERM

3. The appointment of the Distributor shall be for the Initial Period and will continue until terminated by written notice of not less that three months given by either the Distributor or the Principal to the other and expiring at any time after the Initial Period

4. DISTRIBUTOR'S OBLIGATIONS*

4.1 Non-Competition: The Distributor will not without the Principal's prior written consent:
(a) in the Territory directly or indirectly itself or by a connected undertaking manufacture or distribute or deal in any goods which compete with the Products nor obtain the Products other than from the Principal;
(b) outside the Territory:
(i) advertise the Products or canvass or solicit orders for the Products;
(ii) open branches for the sale of the Products
(iii) maintain distribution depots for the Products
but will promptly supply the Principal with full details of all enquiries relating to the supply of the Products to persons outside the Territory

4.2 Duties: The Distributor shall:
(a) use its best efforts to promote and obtain the maximum sales of the Products in the Territory;
(b) retain in the Territory suitable offices, administrative facilities, sales and marketing organisation and engage a sufficient number of competent personnel properly trained to sell, promote [and service] the Products in the Territory;
(c) carry out such customer and end-user training programmes as the principal may from time to time specify;
(d) provide such liaison and support services as the Principal may reasonably request;
(e) at its own expense obtain and retain all necessary permissions, contents and licences to enable the Distributor to import, market, distribute and sell the Products in the Territory and inform the Principal promptly in relation to the same and otherwise take such steps as necessary to enable it at all times lawfully to carry on the business of marketing and supplying the Products;
(f) inform the Principal promptly of any matters which may assist it in assessing the market for Products and similar products to the Products in the Territory;
(g) not change or add to or conceal any markings or packaging supplied by the Principal;

***2.2   This clause is unlikely to be enforceable in respect of major alterations to the products and/or the territory.

*4   If the appointment is for an exclusive distributor to operate in the EEA EC competition law may apply. This precedent complies with the Block Exemption contained in Regulation 1983/83.

(h)   attend at its own expense such events as are agreed or are necessary to promote properly the Products;

(i)   provide to the Principal three months prior to the end of each Contract Period an annual report in the form of Schedule 3 on the activities of the Distributor for the Contract Period and agree with the Principal marketing plans for the following Contract Period;

(j)   not do anything which may prevent the sale or interfere with the development of sales of the Products in the Territory;

(k)   properly store the Products to avoid deterioration and allow the Principal or its representatives access to inspect such storage conditions from time to time upon forty-eight hours' prior notice;

(l)   use its best endeavours to ensure that clearance of the Products through customs and other import formalities into the Territory are carried out as quickly as possible and that the Products are properly stored during such procedure;

(m)   not copy, produce, make, modify or manufacture the Products or any part thereof for use, sale or any other purpose;

(n)   comply with any recommendation of the Principal concerning the safety of the Products (including without limitation their modification, replacement or recall) and procure compliance by its sub-contractors and any third party to whom it has disposed of the Products

5.   SUPPLY OF PRODUCTS

5.1   Terms: The supply of Products to the Distributor will be governed by the Principal's standard terms and conditions of sale as from time to time notified to the Distributor. If there is an inconsistency between such standard terms and conditions and the terms of this appointment the terms of this appointment shall prevail. Each individual order duly accepted shall constitute an individual contract distinct and separate from this appointment

5.2   Product Variations: The Principal reserves the right from time to time to discontinue, modify, replace or otherwise alter the Products or any part of them and the Distributor shall not be entitled to any compensation or other damages in respect of the same

5.3   Price and Payment: The price at which the Product will be sold to the Distributor will be the Distributor List Price less any discount agreed in writing by the Principal and will be paid in the manner specified in Schedule 4. The Principal may charge interest on any overdue sums at the rate of [   ] percentage points above the base rate of [   ] Bank per annum from time to time

5.4   Price Changes: The Principal will give to the Distributor reasonable prior notice of any changes to the Distributor List Price and such changes will apply to deliveries made on or after the expiry date contained in the notice of change unless the order was accepted by the Principal before the date the notice was issued

5.5   No Obligation to Accept Orders: Nothing contained in this appointment obliges the Principal to accept any order placed by the Distributor nor to manufacture or continue the manufacture of the Products nor maintain their availability for sale nor maintain their specifications but the Principal shall not unreasonably refuse to accept an order for Products in current manufacture or stock

6. INTELLECTUAL PROPERTY AND CONFIDENTIAL INFORMATION
Use Clause 6 from the Agency Agreement but replace "Agent" with "Distributor".

7. DISTRIBUTOR'S RECORDS
7. The Distributor shall keep and retain for not less than three years proper accounts together with supporting vouchers (including without limitation copies of invoices and other relevant papers showing all orders for the supply of the Products by the Principal to the Distributor and by the Distributor to its customers) and shall allow the Principal or its authorised representative to inspect, audit and copy the same for the purpose of checking any information given by the Distributor to the Principal or of obtaining any information given by the Distributor to the Principal or of obtaining any information or data relevant to the obligations to be performed by the Distributor under this appointment

8. EARLY TERMINATION
8.1 By Either Party: Either party may at any time terminate this appointment forthwith by written notice to the other if:
(a) the other is in breach of any of the provisions of this appointment and the breach is either incapable of remedy or if it is capable of remedy the other fails to cure it within thirty days of being required by written notice to do so; or
(b) the other becomes insolvent or there is commenced by or against it any procedure which may lead to its liquidation, dissolution, bankruptcy, protection from its creditors or any similar or analogous process under the laws or statutes of any applicable country or state; or
(c) save as provided by Clause 11 the other ceases to do business at any time for thirty or more consecutive business days
8.2 By the Principal: The Principal may at any time terminate this appointment forthwith by notice in writing if there is at any time a material change in the management, ownership or control (where the Distributor is a body corporate as defined in section 840 of the Income and Corporation Taxes Act 1988) of the Distributor
8.3 Accrued Rights: Termination will be without prejudice to any rights and obligations which have accrued prior thereto and to any provision of this appointment intended to take effect upon or continue in effect after termination

9. EFFECT OF TERMINATION
Use Clause 8 from the Agency Agreement but replace "Agent" with "Distributor".

10. NO LIABILITY FOR NON-RENEWAL
10. Non-renewal or termination of this appointment by either party in accordance with its terms shall not give the other any right to compensation, damages, expenditure, loss of profits or prospective profits of any kind or nature whatsoever and in no circumstances shall the Distributor acquire against the Principal any goodwill in respect of the appointment or the Products or their distribution or sale in the Territory or otherwise under or in respect of this appointment

11. FORCE MAJEURE
Use Clause 11 from the Agency Agreement.

12.   INDEMNITY
12.   The Distributor undertakes that it will indemnify and keep indemni-
        fied the Principal for and against all proceedings, costs (including legal
        costs on an indemnity basis), liabilities, injury, loss or damage arising
        from the breach or negligent performance or failure in performance by
        the Distributor of the terms of this Agreement.

13.   GENERAL
13.1   Status: The Distributor acts as principal and as an independent con-
        tractor and is not an agent of the Principal and it has no power to
        bind the Principal or enter into any obligation or make any represen-
        tation or admission on its behalf. Nothing in this agreement shall cre-
        ate a partnership or joint venture between the parties.

*Use Clauses 12.2 to 12.8 from the Agency Agreement replacing "Agent" with
"Distributor" where applicable (and see relevant footnotes).*

IN WITNESS whereof the parties hereto have executed this Agreement the
day and year first before written

The Products

The Products are the products of the Principal listed below:

Name/Description   Mode/Type Number

SCHEDULE 2
The Territory

SCHEDULE 3
Annual Report Format

SCHEDULE 4
Manner of Payment

SIGNED by   )*
[   ]   )
for and on behalf of   )
THE PRINCIPAL in the   )
presence of:)

Witness Name Address and Occupation:

SIGNED by   )
[   ]   )
for and on behalf of   )
THE DISTRIBUTOR in the   )
presence of:)

Witness Name Address and Occupation:

IMPORTANT: This model agreement provides an outline of the types of clauses frequently incorporated in a distribution agreement. Specific legal advice should be sought on the particular facts before entering into such an agreement.

---

*   Execution Clauses: If either of the parties is incorporated or resident overseas, it is important to check that their execution of the agreement complies with the legal requirements for signature of the jurisdiction where they are incorporated or resident.

Excise and Inland Customs Advice Centres

Belfast
Custom House
Queens Square
Belfast BT1 3ET
Tel: 01232 562600
Fax: 01232 562971
Postcodes: BT1–82

Birmingham
HM Customs and Excise
Two Broadway
Broad Street
Five Ways
Birmingham B15 1BG
Tel: 0121-697 4000
Fax: 0121-697 4002
Postcodes: B1–21, 23–38, 40,
42–50, 60–80, 90–98, CV1–13,
21–23, CV31–37, CW3, DY1–14,
GL20, 55, 56, LE1–5, LE7–10,
LE17–18, MK18, 46, NN1–7, 11–13,
OX6, OX15–17, ST1–13, 15–21, TF9,
WR1–14, WS1–15, WV1–16

Bristol
Froomsgate House
Rupert Street
Bristol BS1 2QP
Tel: 0117 900 2000
Fax: 0117 900 2006
Postcodes: BA1–4, 7, 9–15, BS1–25,
99, SN8–15

Cardiff
Excise and Inland Customs Advice
   Centre
Portcullis House
21 Cowbridge Road East
Cardiff CF1 9SS
Tel: 01222 386200
Fax: 01222 386222
Postcodes: A11, CF, NP, SA, LD1–8,
LL35–40, GL15–16, SY23–25

Ipswich
Excise and Inland Customs Advice
   Centre
Haven House
17 Lower Brook Street
Ipswich
Suffolk IP4 1DN
Tel: 01473 235951
Fax: 01473 235921
Postcodes: CB1–11, CM0–9, CO1–16,
IP1–33, NR1–35, PE11–16, 30–38,
SG8–15, SS0–17, 99

London Central
Berkeley House
304 Regents Park Road
Finchley
London N3 2JY
Tel: 0171-865 4400
Fax: 0181-346 9154
Postcodes: E1-3, 5, 8–9, EC1–4,
EN1–9, N2–22, NW1–8, 11, SW1, 3,
5–7, 10, W1–2, 8–11, WC1–2, WD6

Chester
Excise and Inland Customs Advice
   Centre
Eden House
Lakeside
Chester Business Park
Wrexham Road
Chester CH4 9QY
Tel: 01224 684200
Fax: 01224 684299

Dover
Excise and Inland Customs Advice
   Centre
Clarkson House
Rhodaus Town
Canterbury CT1 2JR
Tel: 01227 762255
Fax: 01227 763635
Postcodes: BN20–27, CR3, 5–6,
CT1–21, DA11–13, GU5–6, KT20,
ME1–20, RH1–12, 18, 19, TN1–40

Dundee
Excise and Inland Customs Advice
  Centre
Caledonian House
Greenmarket
Dundee DD1 1HD
Tel: 01382 200822
Fax: 01382 313247
Postcodes: AB1–3, 9, 22–23, 31–32,
34, 37–38, 41–45, 51–56, DD1–11,
HS, PA80–88, PH1–26, 32, 41,
FK1–21, KY1–16, EH1–16, 27–30,
31–46, 51–55, TD1–11, 13, 14,
IV1–28, 30–32, 36, 40–49, 51–56,
ZE1–3, KW1–3, 5–17

Glasgow
Excise and Inland Customs Advice
  Centre
Portcullis House
21 India Street
Glasgow G2 4PZ
Tel: 0141-308 3330/1/2
Fax: 0141-308 3416
Postcodes: G, DG, KA, ML, PA,
PH30–44

Gloucester
Block "B"
Elmbridge Court
Cheltenham Road
Gloucester GL3 1JX
Tel: 01452 306522
Fax: 01452 302258 (VAT)
Fax: 01452 381851 (Excise)
Postcodes: GL1–19, 50–54, HR1–9,
SY1–12, 15–22, SN16, WR15, TF1–8,
10–13

London Port
4th Floor
Jubilee House
2 Farthingale Walk
Stratford
London E15 1AS
Tel: 0181-557 8579
Fax: 0181-557 8570
Postcodes: CM11–16, E2–18, IG1–11,
RM1–18, SS1–17, 99

London South
Advice Centre
South London and Thames
HM Customs and Excise
Dorset House
Stamford Street
London SE1 9PY
Tel: 0171-202 4227
Fax: 0171-202 4216
Postcodes: BR1–8, CM16, CR0, 2, 4,
7–9, DA1–10, 14–18, E4, 6–7, 10–13,
15–18, IG1–11, RM1–18, SE1–28,
SM1, 3–6, SW2, 4, 8–9, 11–20, TW1,
9–10

Manchester
2b Carrs Road
Cheadle
Cheshire SK8 2HW
Tel: 0161-428 3611
Fax: 0161-491 2881
Postcodes: CW4, 8–10, 12, M5, 6,
12–17, 19–23, 29–33, SK1–12, 17,
WA3, 12–16, WN7

Newcastle Upon Tyne
Newcastle Advice Centre
Dobson House
Regent Centre
Gosforth
Newcastle upon Tyne NE3 3PF
Tel: 0191-201 1700
Fax: 0191-201 1742
Postcodes: BD1–24, CA1–28, DH1–9,
DL1–17, DN1–8, 11–12, 14, HD1–8,
HG1–5, HU1–20, HX1–7, LA5–23,
LS1–29, NE1–99, OL14, S63–64,
70–73, SR1–8, TD12(Pt), 15(Pt),
TS1–29, WF1–17, YO1–8, 11–16, 17,
18, 21–22, 25

North West England
North West Advice Centre
Boundary House
Cheadle Point
Cheadle
Cheshire SK8 2JZ
Tel: 0161-912 7300
Fax: 0161-912 7399
Postcodes: FY1–8, BB1–12, BL1–7,
L1–49, 60–66, PR1–9. WA1–2, 4–11,
WN1–6, 8

Nottingham
Bowman House
100–102 Talbot Street
Nottingham NG1 5NG
Tel: 0115 971 2219
Fax: 0115 948 3487
Postcodes: AL1–10, DE1–7, 11–15,
21–24, 45, 55–56, 65, 72–75,
DN1–12, 14–22, 31–40, HP2, LE6,
11–16, 65, 67, LN1–13, LU1–7,
MK1–17, 19, 40–45, NG1–25, 31–34,
NN8–10, 14–18, PE1–11, 17–19,
20–25, S1–14, 17–19, 30–31, S40–45,
49, 60–66, 70–75, 80–81, SG16–19,
ST14

Oldham
Oliver House
Oliver Street
Oldham
Tel: 0161-652 0621
Fax: 0161-912 6699
Postcodes: BB1–12, BL0–9, M1–4,
7–11, 18, 24–28, 34, 35, 60, OL1–13,
15, 16, SK13–16

Plymouth
Excise and Inland Customs Advice
  Centre
Crownhill Court
Tailyour Road
Crownhill
Plymouth PL6 5Z
Tel: 01752 777123
Fax: 01752 765807

Reading
Excise and Inland Customs Advice
  Centre
Thames Valley Collection
Eldon Court
75 London Road
Reading
Berks RG1 5BS
Tel: 0118 964 4200
Fax: 0118 964 4208
Postcodes: GU1–4, 7–25, HA0–9, HP1,
3–23, 27, KT1–19, 21–24, NW9–10,
OX1–5, 7–14, 18, 20, 33, 44,˙
RG1–31, 40–42, 45, SL0–9, SM2, 7,
SN1–9, TW2–8, 11–20, UB1–11,
W2–7, 12–14, WD1–5, 7

Redhill
Excise and Inland Customs Advice
  Centre
Warwick House
67 Station Road
Redhill
Surrey RH1 1QU
Tel: 0845 199199
Fax: 01737 734600

Southampton
Excise Advice Centre
Custom House
Orchard Place
Southampton SO14 3NS
Tel: 01703 827068
Fax: 01703 827048
Postcodes: BH1–25, BN1–18,
GU26–35, PO1–41, RH13–17, 20,
SO1–52, SP1–6, 9–11

Government departments

GSP Agricultural and Industrial Schemes
Bay 340, DTI
Kingsgate House
66–74 Victoria Street
London SW1E 6SW
Tel: 0171 215 4552/4254
Fax: 0171 215 4539

Gatt and Tariff Quotas
Trade Policy and Europe Directorate
Bay 310, DTI
Kingsgate House
66–74 Victoria Street
London SW1E 6SW
Tel: 0171 215 4548/9
Fax: 0171 215 4249

Central Tariff Quota Unit
HM Customs and Excise Operations
  and Compliance Directorate 4A
1st Floor, North West
CE Heath House
61–71 Victoria Avenue
Southend on Sea SS2 6EY
Tel: 01702 361-979
Fax: 01702 361-975

Department of Trade and Industry
Kingsgate House
67–74 Victoria Street
London SW1E 6SW
Tel: 0171 215 5000

Department of Trade and Industry
Small Firms and Business Links
  Division
St Mary's House, Level 1
c/o Moorfoot
Sheffield S1 4PG
Tel: 0114 259 7308/9
Fax: 0114 259 7316

Duty Deferment
HM Customs and Excise
R1204, Portcullis House
27 Victoria Avenue
Southend on Sea SS2 6AL
Tel: 01702 367425
Fax: 01702 366091

HM Customs and Excise HQ
New King's Beam House
22 Upper Ground
London SE1 9PJ
Tel: 0171 620 1313
Fax: 0171 202 4131

Import Licensing Information
Import Licensing Branch
DTI
Queensway House
West Precinct
Billingham
Cleveland TS23 2NF
Tel: 0642 364333/4
Fax: 0642 533557

Rules of Origin Information
Department of Trade and Industry
TPE 3C
Kingsgate House
66–74 Victoria Street
London SW1E 6SW
Tel: 0171 215 4491/4557
Fax: 0171 215 4556

Tariff and Statistical Office
HM Customs and Excise
TGC 13, Room 503
Portcullis House
27 Victoria Avenue
Southend on Sea SS2 6AL
Tel: 01702 348944
Fax: 01702 367343

Traders registering for VAT and the import of goods from outside the EU need a trader's unique reference number (TURN). To obtain one write to:

TURN Team
HM Customs and Excise
R 407, Portcullis House
27 Victoria Avenue
Southend on Sea SS2 6AL
Tel: 01702 366425/7
Fax: 01702 367097

For preferential rates of CAP duties contact:

Intervention Board for Agricultural Products
Lancaster House
Hampshire Court
Newcastle upon Tyne NE4 7YE
Tel: 0191 273 9696
Fax: 0191 273 1839

Contact points for certain import restrictions

Agricultural, horticultural and food products
Intervention Board for Agricultural Produce
Lancaster House
Hampshire Court
Newcastle upon Tyne NE4 7YE
Tel: 0191 273 9696
Fax: 0191 226 1839

Animal health requirements
Ministry of Agriculture, Fisheries and Food
Animal Health Division
Hook Rise South
Tolworth
Surbiton
Surrey KT6 7NF

(Livestock)   Tel: 0181 330 8196
              Fax: 0181 330 6678

(Domestic
pets)   Tel: 0181 330 8174
              Fax: 0181 330 3640

Drugs
Home Office
Drugs Branch Licensing Section
50 Queen Anne's Gate
London SW1H 9AT
Tel: 0171 273 3147
Fax: 0171 273 2671

Endangered species
Department of the Environment
Tollgate House
Houlton Street
Bristol BS2 9DJ
Tel: 0117 987 8170/6165
Fax: 0117 987 8642

Explosives (including ammunition and fireworks)
Health and Safety Executive
Explosives Inspectorate
(THSDA3)
Room 443, Magdalen House
Staley Precinct
Bootle
Merseyside L20 3QZ
Tel: 0151 951 4025
Fax: 0151 951 3891

Plant health requirements
Plant Health Division
Ministry of Agriculture, Fisheries
   and Food
R 340, Foss House
Kings Pool
1–2 Pebsholme Green
York YO1 2DY
Tel: 01904 455191/2
Fax: 01904 455199

Plant Health and Potatoes Branch
Scottish Office Department of
Agriculture and Fisheries
Pentland House
47 Robb's Loan
Edinburgh EH14 1TY
Tel: 0131 556 8400

Public health requirements
Ministry of Agriculture, Fisheries
   and Food
Meat Hygiene Division
11th Floor, Tolworth Tower
Tolworth
Surbiton
Surrey KT6 7DX
Tel: 0181 330 4411
exts 8339/8340/8341/8342
Fax: 0181 337 3640/0181 330 1563

Radio transmitting devices
Department of Trade and Industry
Radiocommunications Agency
New King's Beam House
22 Upper Ground
London SE1 9PJ
Tel: 0171 211 0211
Fax: 0171 608 3985

DTI Country Desks

Kingsgate House
66-74 Victoria Street
London SW1 6SW
Tel: 0171 215 5000

Asia Pacific

Japan
Tel: 0171 215 4801

South Korea
Tel: 0171 215 4809

Indonesia
Tel: 0171 215 4886

The Philippines
Tel: 0171 215 8743

Singapore
Tel: 0171 215 8479

Malaysia
Tel: 0171 215 4865

Brunei
Tel: 0171 215 8479

Thailand
Tel: 0171 215 4924

China, Hong Kong
Tel: 0171 215 4957

Taiwan
Tel: 0171 215 4729

Australasia

Australia
Tel: 0171 215 4916

New Zealand
Tel: 0171 215 4916

Central and Eastern Europe

Albania, Bulgaria, Croatia, Romania,
Slovenia, former Yugoslavia
Tel: 0171 215 4812

Ukraine, Belarus, Moldova
Tel: 0171 215 4257/5265

Armenia, Azerbaijan, Georgia,
Kazakhstan, Kyrgystan, Tajikistan,
Turkmenistan, Uzbekistan
Tel: 0171 215 2671/2681

Czech and Slovak Republics,
Hungary, Poland
Tel: 0171 215 8194

Latin America and the Caribbean

Argentina
Tel: 0171 215 4959

Brazil
Tel: 0171 215 4893

The Caribbean
Tel: 0171 215 4763

Chile, Paraguay
Tel: 0171 215 8031

Colombia
Tel: 0171 215 4989

Guatemala
Tel: 0171 215 8274

Ecuador, Peru, Bolivia
Tel: 0171 215 8170

Mexico
Tel: 0171 215 4297

Uruguay
Tel: 0171 215 4959

Venezuela
Tel: 0171 215 4820

Middle East and North Africa

Morocco
Tel: 0171 215 8326

Tunisia
Tel: 0171 215 8434

Bahrain, Qatar
Tel: 0171 215 4961

Oman
Tel: 0171 215 4388

Saudi Arabia
Tel: 0171 215 4852

Malta
Tel: 0171 215 8216

Syria
Tel: 0171 215 4976

Turkey
Tel: 0171 215 8332

Iran
Tel: 0171 215 4367

Egypt
Tel: 0171 215 4947

United Arab Emirates
Tel: 0171 215 4329

Cyprus
Tel: 0171 215 4958

Israel
Tel: 0171 215 4949

Jordan
Tel: 0171 215 8461

North America

Trade promotions

USA
Tel: 0171 215 8145

Canada
Tel: 0171 215 4822

South Asia

Pakistan
Tel: 0171 215 4777

India
Tel: 0171 215 8116

Bangladesh
Tel: 0171 215 4836

Sub-Saharan Africa

Zimbabwe
Tel: 0171 215 4818

Kenya
Tel: 0171 215 4926

Tanzania
Tel: 0171 215 4973

Ethiopia, Eritrea
Tel: 0171 215 4973

Nigeria
Tel: 0171 215 4968

Ghana
Tel: 0171 215 4969

Uganda
Tel: 0171 215 4926

South Africa
Tel: 0171 215 4813

Swaziland
Tel: 0171 215 8471

Côte D'Ivoire
Tel: 0171 215 4967

Western Europe

Austria, Liechtenstein, Switzerland
Tel: 0171 215 4798

Belgium, Luxembourg
Tel: 0171 215 4794

Netherlands
Tel: 0171 215 4790

Denmark
Tel: 0171 215 8657

Norway
Tel: 0171 215 8267

Sweden
Tel: 0171 215 4731

Finland
Tel: 0171 215 4783

France
Tel: 0171 215 4942

Iceland
Tel: 0171 215 8267

Germany
Tel: 0171 215 4995

Greece
Tel: 0171 215 4774

Republic of Ireland
Tel: 0171 215 4782

Spain
Tel: 0171 215 4357

Italy
Tel: 0171 215 4785

Portugal
Tel: 0171 215 4721

Simpler Trade Procedures Board services

SITPRO
161 Buckingham Palace Road
London SW1W 9SS
Tel: 0171 215 0825/0800
Fax: 0171 215 0824

Overseas countries' Chambers of Commerce in the UK

American Chamber of Commerce
   (UK)
75 Brook Street
London W1Y 2EB
Tel: 0171 493 0381
Fax: 0171 493 2394

Arab British Chamber of Commerce
6 Belgrave Square
London SW1X 8PH
Tel: 0171 235 4363
Fax: 0171 245 6688

Australian British Chamber of
   Commerce
Morley House
314-322 Regent Street
London WlR 5AE
Tel: 0171 636 4525
Fax: 0171 636 4511

British Bulgarian Chamber of
   Commerce
186 Queens Gate
London SW7
Tel: 0171 584 8333

Belgian Luxembourg Chamber of
   Commerce
73 Upper Richmond Road
London SW15 2SZ

Brazilian Chamber of Commerce
   and Economic Affairs in Great
   Britain
32 Green Street
London W1Y 4AT
Tel: 0171 499 0186
Fax: 0171 493 4621

Canada-United Kingdom Chamber
   of Commerce
38 Grosvenor Street
London W1X 0DP

British Argentine Chamber of
Commerce
Canning House
2 Belgrave Square
London SW1X 8BJ
Tel: 0171 245 6661
Fax: 0171 235 7013

Danish-United Kingdom Chamber
of Commerce
55 Sloane Street
London SW1X 9SR
Tel: 0171 259 6795
Fax: 0171 333 0243

Egyptian-British Chamber of
Commerce
Kent House, Market Place
London W1A 4EG
Tel: 0171 323 2856
Fax: 0171 323 5739

French Chamber of Commerce in
Great Britain
Knightsbridge House
197 Knightsbridge
London SW7 1RB
Tel: 0171 304 4040
Fax: 0171 304 7034

German British Chamber of
Commerce and Industry in the UK
Mecklenburg House
16 Buckingham Gate
London SW1E 6LB
Tel: 0171 233 5656
Fax: 0171 233 7835

Italian Chamber of Commerce for
Great Britain
Walmar House
296 Regent Street
London W1R 5HB
Tel: 0171 637 3153
Fax: 0171 436 6037

Japanese Chamber of Commerce
and Industry (UK)
Salisbury House, 2nd Floor
29 Finsbury Circus
London EC2M 5QQ
Tel: 0171 628 0069
Fax: 0171 628 0248

Netherlands-British Chamber of
Commerce
The Dutch House
307-308 High Holborn
London WC1V 7LS
Tel: 0171 405 1358/242 1064
Fax: 0171 405 1689

New Zealand UK Chamber of
Commerce
Morley House
314-322 Regent Street
London W1R 5AE
Tel: 0171 636 4525
Fax: 0171 636 4511

Nigerian British Chamber of
Commerce
PO Box 338
Thatcham
Newbury
Berkshire RG18 0YY
Tel: 01635 200799
Fax: 01635 200799

Norwegian British Chamber of
Commerce
Norway House
21-24 Cockspur Street
London SW1Y 5BN
Tel: 0171 930 0181
Fax: 0171 930 7946

British Polish Chamber of
Commerce
55 Exhibition Road
London SW7 2PG
Tel: 0171 591 0057
Fax: 0171 591 0067

Portuguese Chamber of Commerce
and Industry
4th Floor
22-25a Sackville Street
London W1X 1DE
Tel: 0171 494 1844
Fax: 0171 494 1822

Russo-British Chamber of Commerce
42 Southwark Street
London SE1 1UN
Tel: 0171 403 4577
Fax: 0171 403 3691

Spanish Chamber of Commerce
5 Cavendish Square
London W1M 6DP
Tel: 0171 637 9061
Fax: 0171 436 7188

Swedish Chamber of Commerce
73 Welbeck Street
London W1M 7HA
Tel: 0171 486 4545
Fax: 0171 935 5487

Turkish-British Chamber of
   Commerce and Industry
89 Goswell Road
London EC1V 7ER
Tel: 0171 336 0686
Fax: 0171 336 0696

Trade development organizations

Argentina Commercial Department
111 Cadogan Gardens
London SW3 2RQ
Tel: 0171 730 9334

Austrian Trade Commission
45 Princes Gate
London SW7 2QA
Tel: 0171 584 4411

Australian Trade Commission
(Austrade)
Australia House
Strand
London WC2B 4LA
Tel: 0171 887 S326
Fax: 0171 836 4250

Brazilian Trade Centre
32 Green Street
London W1Y 4AT
Tel: 0171 499 0877

China Britain Trade Group
Abford House
15 Wilton Road
London SW1V lLT
Tel: 0171 828 S176

Danish Trade Office
55 Sloane Square
London SW1X 9SR
Tel: 0171 333 0200

East European Trade Council
10 Westminster Palace Gardens
Artillery Row
London SW1P 1RL
Tel: 0171 222 7622

Finland Trade Centre
30 Pall Mall
London SW1Y 5LP
Tel: 0171 747 3000

Hong Kong Trade Development
   Council
Swire House
59 Buckingham Gate
London SW1E 6AJ
Tel: 0171 828 1661
Fax: 0171 828 9976

Indonesia Trade Promotions Centre
Sherbourne House
13 Savile Row
London W1X 1AE
Tel: 0171 439 0189/0767

Irish Trade Board
Ireland House
150 New Bond Street
London W1Y 0HD
Tel: 0171 3S5 1555

Italian Trade Centre
37 Sackville Street
London W1X 2DQ
Tel: 0171 734 2412
Fax: 0171 734 2Sl6

JETRO London
(Japan External Trade Organisation)
Leconfield House
Curzon Street
London W1Y 8LQ
Tel: 0170 470 4700

Korea Trade Centre
39 St James's Street
London SW1A 1JD
Tel: 0171 491 8057

LATAG
(Latin American Trade Advisory
Group)
Canning House
2 Belgrave Square
London SW1X 8PJ
Tel: 0171 235 3651/259 6276

Malaysian Trade Commission
17 Curzon Street
London W1Y 7FE
Tel: 0171 499 7388/5908
Fax: 0171 493 3199

Middle East Association
Bury House
33 Bury Street
London SW1Y 6AX
Tel: 0171 839 2137
Fax: 0171 839 6121

New Zealand Trade Development
    Board
80 Haymarket
London SW1Y 4TE
Tel: 0171 973 0380
Fax: 0171 973 0104

Norwegian Trade Council
Charles House
Lower Regent Street
London SW1Y 4LR
Tel: 0171 973 0188

Portuguese Trade and Tourism
    Office
4th Floor
22-25a Sackville Street
London W1X 2EA
Tel: 0171 494 1517

Singapore Trade Development Board
5 Chesham Street
London SW1X 8ND
Tel: 0171 235 4558
Fax: 0171 235 4557

Swedish Trade Council
73 Welbeck Street
London W1M 8AN
Tel: 0171 935 9601

Taiwan Trade Centre
3rd Floor
29 Wilson Street
London EC2M 2SJ
Tel: 0171 638 4676
Fax: 0171 638 4686

Other useful addresses

British Importers Association Ltd
Suite B
Castle House
25 Castlereagh Street
London W1H 5YR
Tel: 0171 258 3999
Fax: 0171 724 5055

British International Freight
  Association (BIFA) and Institute of
  Freight Forwarders (IFF)
Redfern House
Browells Lane
Feltham
Middlesex TV13 7EP
Tel: 0181 844 2266
Fax: 0181 890 S546

British Standards Institution
(Standards and Specifications)
389 Chiswick High Road
London W4 4AL
Tel: 0181 996 9000
Fax: 0181 996 7048

Business Cooperation Centre (BCC)
89 Rue Froissard
B-1040 Brussels
Belgium
Tel: 00 322 2304091/2303949

CCN Group
Abbey House
Abbeyfield Road
Lenton
Nottingham NG7 2SW
Tel: 0115 986 3864
Fax: 0115 964 3517

Centre for International Briefing
The Castle
Farnham
Surrey GU9 0AG
Tel: 01252 721194
Fax: 01252 711283

Chartered Institute of Purchasing
  and Supply
Easton House
Easton on the Hill
Stamford
Lincolnshire PE9 3NZ

Tel: 01780 756777
Fax: 01780 751610

Chartered Institute of Transport
(CIT)
80 Portland Place
London W1N 4DP
Tel: 0171 636 9952
Fax: 0171 637 0511

The Crafts Council
44a Pentonville Road
London N1 9BY
Tel: 0171 278 7700
Fax: 0171 837 6891

DECTA
(Developing Countries Trade
  Agency)
Bank House
1-7 Sutton Court Road
Sutton
Surrey SM1 4SP
Tel: 0181 643 3311
Fax: 0181 643 8030

Design Council (Consultancy
  Division)
34 Bow Street
London WC2E 7DL
Tel: 0171 420 5200
Fax: 0171 420 5300

Dun & Bradstreet Ltd
Holmers Farm Way
High Wycombe
Buckinghamshire HP12 4UL
Tel: 01494 422000
Fax: 01494 422260

Electronic Commerce Association
Ramillies House
1-9 Hills Place
London W1R 1AG
Tel: 0171 432 2500
Fax: 0171 432 2501

Commission of European
  Communities
8 Storey's Gate
London SW1P 3AT
Tel: 0171 973 1992
Fax: 0171 973 1900

European Investment Bank (EIB)
8 Pall Mall
London SW1Y SES
Tel: 0171 839 3351
Fax: 0171 930 9929

European Venture Capital
    Association (EVCA)
Keiberg Park
Minervastraat 6
B-1930 Zaventen
Belgium
Tel: 00 322 720 6010
Fax: 00 322 725 3036

Export Services Directorate
Department of Trade and Industry
Kingsgate House
66–74 Victoria Street
London SW1E 6SW
Tel: 0171 215 2400
Fax: 0171 215 2424

FIATA
Represented by BIFA in the UK;
address on page 124

Graydon International
Hyde House
Edgware Road
London NW9 6LW
Tel: 0181 975 1050
Fax: 0181 975 1099/1994

Institute of Chartered Shipbrokers
3 St Helen's Place
London EC3A 6BJ
Tel: 0171 628 5559
Fax: 0171 688 5445

Institute of Packaging
Sysonby Lodge
Nottingham Road
Melton Mowbray
Leicestershire LE13 0NU
Tel: 01664 500055
Fax: 01664 64164

International Chamber of
    Commerce (ICC)
14 Belgrave Square
London SW1X 8PX
Tel: 0171 823 2811
Fax: 0171 23S 5447

Pira International (packaging)
Randalls Road
Leatherhead
Surrey KT22 7RU
Tel: 01372 376161
Fax: 01372 360104

SGS United Kingdom Ltd
Gaw House
Alperton Lane
Wembley
London HA8 1WU
Tel: 0181 998 2171
Fax: 0181 991 6844

Special publications and directories

Special publications

Croner's Reference Book for Importers
Croner Publications Ltd
Croner House
London Road
Kingston upon Thames
Surrey KT2 6SR
Tel: 0181 547 3333
Fax: 0181 547 2637

Customs Tariff and Overseas Trade
  Classifications Public Notices
HM Customs and Excise
New King's Beam House
22 Upper Ground
London SE1 9PJ
Tel: 0171 620 1313

Individual Country Hints to
  Exporters and Country Profiles
EMIC Library
Department of Trade and Industry
Kingsgate House
66–74 Victoria Street
London SW1E 6SW
Tel: 0171 215 5444/5
Fax: 0171 215 4321

International Certification and
  Approval Schemes Booklet
British Standards Institute
Linford Wood
Milton Keynes
MK14 6LE
Tel: 01908 221166
Fax: 01908 220671

Lloyd's List and other publications
69–77 Paul Street
London EC2A 4LQ
Tel: 0171 553 1000
Fax: 0171 250 0998

UK Importers - customised lists
Business and Trade Statistics Ltd
Lancaster House
More Lane
Esher
Surrey KT10 8AP
Tel: 01372 463121
Fax: 01372 469847

Directories

The Caribbean Yellow Pages
Caribbean Yellow Pages

The Dawson Top 3000 Directories and
Annuals
Dawson UK Ltd

Directory of British Importers
British Importers Confederation

Directory of Directories
Gale Research

Directory of East European Business
Mercury Books

Directory of European Industrial Trade
Associations
CBD Research

Directory of International Trade Fairs
and Exhibitions
MNA

European Directory of Trade and
Business Associations
Euromonitor

International Directory of Importers
Interdate

International Trade Show Directory
M&A Publications

Kompass Country Directories
Kompass Publications

Major Business Organisations of
Eastern European and the CIS
Graham and Trotman

Major Companies of the Arab World
Graham and Trotman

National Freight and Transport Guide
Commercial Publications

Tradeshows Worldwide
Gale Research

World Directory of Exhibitions and
Trade Fairs
Euromonitor

Index